CONSULTIVE SELLING

CLOSE MORE SALES, BUILD TRUST AND IMPROVE CUSTOMER LOYALTY THROUGH AUTHENTIC SALES PROCESSES AND SKILLS

JOHN BRENNAN

ISBN: 1-4392-2857-4
ISBN-13: 9781439228579

Visit www.booksurge.com to order additional copies.

FOREWORD

The purpose of this book is to educate and inform sales reps, sales managers and VPs about the reasons you should take a second look at the way you approach selling in the new global age and to suggest some new strategies and polish up some age old skills to enable a change.

The book comes as a result of twenty-five years of coaching and training sales people to sell, while selling the moving target of my own company's services. Friends, colleagues and customers have urged me to put down on paper what I know to be true about this dynamic profession.

If you believe that the business world is changing, that the way customers buy is changing, and that the profession of selling is changing, this is the book for you. If you have a thorough understanding of the forces of change affecting your industry and your profession and if you are willing to take a hard look at some assumptions about selling that may have served you well yesterday, then read on. The benefits of doing so will be enormous. The new world belongs to those who welcome change, who ride the crest of change, and who understand that change, not stability, is the natural state of things. The sales forces of most companies will shrink, and at the same time, the responsibilities and rewards of those that remain will expand. The rewards will go to the authentic, well-prepared, well trained sales reps who can empathize with their customers on a number of levels while truly representing the capabilities of the companies they work for and the industry they sell in.

You should read this book if you work inside a small, medium or large organization. Your sales organization may be organized along customer industry lines, product lines or geography. Your job title may be sales representative, account executive, sales consultant, customer relationship manager, business development executive, sales manager, regional sales manager, national sales manager, sales director or vice-president of sales. Perhaps you do not have a sales person job title but part of your role is bringing in new business. Perhaps you are involved in developing accounts and playing the role of technical expert in the sales process. You may be an independent sales rep, or the owner of a small business. Consultants, lawyers, accountants, health care professionals in private practice - you all sell your services. If so, this book is also for you.

ABOUT THE AUTHOR

John Brennan, Ed.D

Dr. John Brennan has focused his career on sales training - designing and delivering sales training programs in North America, Asia, Europe, Australia, and the Middle East. His specific expertise includes sales management, sales skills enhancement, business development, sales coaching, and instructional design.

Dr. Brennan received his doctorate from the University of Rochester where his dissertation researched the effects of training on the development of empathy.

To help a European auto manufacturer launch its most successful new product in history, he designed and delivered a global sales training program. He recruited, trained and managed sales trainers to deliver the courses. Other sales training clients have included Gannett Company, Pharmacia, Prudential, Standard Register, and Volkswagen.

Dr. Brennan has developed the selling skills of hundreds of sales reps and managers in intense, small group, interactive, classroom-style courses. As a trainer/facilitator, he has achieved outstanding participant satisfaction ratings.

He is also the publisher of Sales Coaching Matters, a monthly newsletter and is a member of the United Professional Sales Association and the American Society for Training and Development.

ACKNOWLEDGEMENTS

Thank you to the thousands of my clients around the world who have taken my sales training courses and shared their experiences with me. Your questions, concerns, problems and challenges inspired and informed this book.

Thanks also to Larry Newman at Shipley Associates, Dr. Ken Rabinowitz at the Professional Development Group, John Hansell, formerly at Interpersonal Development Ltd. and the creators of MarketingMO at Moderandi Inc. for opening my eyes to new perspectives on selling and the sales process. If my writing is at all engaging, special thanks are due to Kathi Albertini at Management Growth Inc., Walt MacEachern and Jim Demoux at Shipley Associates and Roz Hooke, formerly at Gannett, Inc.

I will be forever grateful to my wife, Johanna, who never stops believing in me.

TABLE OF CONTENTS

CHAPTER 1:
THE EVOLUTION OF SELLING

*And for a salesman, there is no rock bottom to
the life. He's a man way out there in the blue,
riding on a smile and a shoeshine.*
- Arthur Miller, Death of a Salesman.

Selling began with the birth of civilization and
has grown up with it. While selling has been a
central activity in our world, computers, global
competition, the migration from the industrial age
to the information age and now to the global age, have
changed the way customers buy. The Pharaohs in Ancient
Egypt used the military to coerce their neighbors into
trading with them and facilitated deals by using coins to
represent stores of grain. If you were a buyer, you accepted
the deal the Pharaoh offered you and you were grateful for it.

By the middle ages in Europe, buyers had more choices as
the emerging merchant class had gathered some power for
itself and established the first rules of the market. The village
elders designated an area in the center of the village, or in
the shadow of the cathedral or temple as the marketplace.
Certain days of the week were designated market days and
merchants were assigned locations where they could park
their wheelbarrows and wagons. In this marketplace, the
merchants who could sell and negotiate the best were the
most successful. They relied on their personal charisma,
shrewdness and persistence to close deals. Buyers learned
to shop around for the best deal, and all were very aware of
the meaning of "caveat emptor". Remnants of this model
can still be seen today in the farmer's markets in the US and
Europe and in the bazaars of the Middle East.

Soon the industrial revolution changed the local marketplace
by introducing big business and flooding the market with

manufactured goods. Buyers had more money and they chased the new manufactured goods. Over the next 200 years selling became largely a matter of order-taking. If you worked long hours and made lots of sales calls you made a lot of sales. It became a numbers game; in fact some industries could tell you exactly how many qualified candidates you should call to reach a target number of sales. You demonstrated your products, pointed out their features and benefits, overcame any objections and then closed the sale. If your customer did not buy, you were encouraged to make a second effort. If that did not work, well, onto the next qualified candidate. There was an unlimited supply and they all needed your product.

You could also be successful in this environment by leveraging relationships. You joined the country club, you networked with friends and associates, you turned on your charming personality and sales started to roll in. By nurturing the relationship you could lock out the competition and get repeat orders forever.

Then along came the Internet and global competition and the world developed an insatiable appetite for information and the technology to manage it. Your customer's supply chain now stretches back into emerging nations who produce manufactured goods for less than western countries. Your multinational customer may have a purchasing manager in London, a decision-maker in Shanghai and end users in Dubai, all who communicate with each other instantly. You can no longer just "propose and close" or depend on a relationship to win. You have to add significant value to the sale process or risk being replaced by a streamlined, lower cost supply chain.

Today the emerging global age is establishing new rules for goods, services and relationships. Governments are banding together to ensure that products respect and protect the environment while also ensuring that traders respect and protect human rights. In the USA, voters are calling for transparency and honesty in government. Politicians who practice and promote authentic government and authentic relationships are wildly popular. In the marketplace, buyers will expect similar authenticity of you and your selling practices, adding a new dimension to your standard sales processes and techniques.

Wikipedia defines authenticity as the degree to which one is true to one's own personality spirit, or character. A century of books on selling have encouraged you to acquire selling techniques and attitudes to close the sale. They advise a sunny disposition and an enthusiastic approach to sales. Few, if any, show you how to practice these characteristics without losing your authentic self. You risk being perceived as, at best an actor, and at worst, a phony. Often you seem to walk the thin line between truth and dishonesty, between influencing your customer and manipulating them, and between honoring the trust your customer has placed in you and betraying it. The purpose of this book is to show you how to skillfully sell today's customers by removing the phony mask and allowing your customer to experience the authentic you. But as a first step, consider the effects of global and technological change on the buying habits and expectations of customers.

Customers today are better educated, better informed, better trained and have higher expectations from the people who call on them. They have access to unlimited information and buying tools and simply have less need for you, the traditional sales person. In *Business to Business (B2B)* sales, the Internet enables your customer to shop prices with auctions and reverse auctions. Supplier selection has become a very sophisticated process that has virtually shut out your traditional sales role. If you have retained your sales job, its title may include the word "manager" or "consultant", but probably not "sales rep". You don't close sales; you simply manage the sales process like any other business process. You manage the big deals and the big accounts. The small deals and the small accounts are handled by advanced tools on your company's web site or are outsourced to a telemarketing firm. The traditional outside sales rep's activities no longer exist.

Telesales, direct marketing and online shopping are eroding the traditional territory and function of outside sales reps. The Internet enables customers to reduce the time they need face to face with sales people to get information and, when dealing with small or repeat orders, to try to eliminate it altogether. When your customers want to see a sales rep today, they expect to see an executive, someone who can empathize, problem-solve, put together and manage a large and complex order. They may refuse to see an order-taker, a product-pusher, or a relationship builder. Your customers do not have the time to spend educating you about their company's mission, customers, products and business issues - they expect you to already know that. Your customers expect you to listen to their specific needs and partner with them to tailor your solution or create a new one.

Your customers do not want to be "sold". They want you to be authorized to close a deal and take the order when they are ready to give it. Beyond that, unless you can add significant value by deepening their understanding of their problem, by tailoring your solution or by streamlining their purchasing process, you are wasting their time.

Your customers are paying more attention to *return on investment* (ROI) and differentiating the value of the products and services they purchase. They are looking for value in your solution or, if they perceive your product as a commodity, then they look for the lowest price. Purchasing managers are knowledgeable about sophisticated decision-making models and are trained in negotiating skills.

Your multi-national customers may be buying for their worldwide operations. If you want to do business with them you must be well informed about the global marketplace and their global needs, and show understanding of, and sensitivity to gender, cultural, ethnic, racial and national differences. The person across the desk from you may not belong to the same ethnic or national background as you. Customers buy from people they like – and it is easier to like someone who is like them. Failing that, customers look for people who respect and even enjoy differences. Become a student of local, regional, national and cultural differences. Understand them and respect them. Regardless of background, your customers will find it easier to like you, trust you and buy from the authentic you.

CHAPTER 2:
WHAT CUSTOMERS WANT

*Earn the Right to Close
through Understanding*

Today your customers can place orders on a web site or through e-purchasing. They can order via telephone, email, fax or instant messaging and consumers can visit retail stores. Your customers expect to shop and buy efficiently while understanding that buying is a process that varies in length and that they must choose among a myriad of products and sales channels.

In survey after survey, when customers are asked what they want in a sales person, they emphatically state that they want you to know your products. According to a Cahners Survey, 58% of buyers say sales reps are unable to answer their questions effectively. Customers will forgive you for a lot of things, but they won't forgive you if you do not know your own company's products. Competency in answering questions about your company and product's capabilities is the chief qualification for admission to the customer's office. It will not guarantee you an order, but it will get you respect from the customer, and an opportunity to use your selling skills to get an order.

Equally important to your customer is that you should know your industry. They expect you to be fully aware of industry trends, the major players, your key competitors, emerging technology, and innovations in customer purchasing. They expect you to educate them about the impact of these factors on their business. They want to know how their competitors are responding to change; are they jumping right in or are they taking a wait-and-see stance? They expect you to understand, and have a viewpoint on alternative solutions to their problems. Are there experimental or emerging products that some day may replace the products they are buying today? Are there alternative delivery methods? Are there any companies outsourcing or bringing inside the services or functions you are selling? What industry publications might be of interest to them? They want you to know and freely share this information.

By keeping your customers up to date on these and other issues, you reinforce your position as an authentic sales person, and reassure your customers that they are doing business with the best company available.

Your customers also expect you to be familiar with their company, especially if they are a leader in their industry or a prominent company in the local community. You should know about your customer's main products or services, the industry groups they sell to, their best customers and their position in the market. You should be aware of the locations of their major manufacturing, distribution and regional offices, their approximate size in revenue, employees or industry ranking, divisional structure and names of any subsidiary companies. You should be conversant with current issues in their industry, any current public issues in their company and the name of their CEO. There are no excuses for lack of preparation; you can get most of the information through a search engine or the customer's own website.

Today's customers expect you to wear many hats. In your *business consultant* role customers expect you to be knowledgeable about your industry and your products, as well as your customer's needs, markets, and business objectives. You should be able to carry on an informed conversation with your customer about key issues. You should be able to identify the value suppliers, manufacturers, distributors and retailers add to products and services and trace the flow of money through business. You should understand key financial terms including revenue, operating expenses, cost of goods, gross profit, ROI and standard financial reports. You must appreciate the contributions of Manufacturing, Finance, HR, IT, Quality, Customer Service, Marketing and Sales to business success. You also must develop sensitivity to typical small business concerns including cash flow, recruiting and retention of staff, venture capital financing, and expansion through going public, merging or acquiring other businesses. If you acquire this knowledge and use it authentically in the service of your customer you will become a *trusted advisor*.

You must also wear the hat of a strategic *partner* with your customer, with shared long-term business interests which include making your customer a hero. Build a strong relationship with your customer that will mitigate your inevitable mistakes and which will open many doors of opportunity. You should be so valuable as a partner that you become one of the benefits your customers fight to keep! You must excel as a *leader,* encouraging exchanges of information and relationship building while managing the buying process for your customer and your team. Build a network of key players in your accounts, and in your company, so that you can synchronize your sales process with your customer's buying process - all while helping your company take on complex and profitable accounts. Become your *customer's advocate* within your company, seeing to it that their orders are processed and delivered on time and that key managers in your company know and value your customer. To create an atmosphere that makes selling an enjoyable and frequent activity for you and your buyers become a *cheerleader* for your customer. Combine persistence and optimism to keep you and your customer moving forward and to make it through the down turns.

Your customers want you to be authentic in your dealings with them. Most abhor the "hard sell" which is rarely effective with large ticket, business-to-business sales. The "hard sell" approach might close the deal, but with a negative effect on life-time customer value and the integrity of the seller. For example, consider the following case of a firm that provides general business consulting to small businesses – primarily "Mom and Pops". In ten years they have experienced rapid growth, in the neighborhood of 50% and more each year. Annual revenues are well over $100 million and they have thousands of employees. Their telephone sales reps cold call business owners, manipulating and lying to them to get the appointment, the sales reps pressure the owner into a "free" business analysis, sometimes lying about the expertise of the business analyst, and the business analysts close on high-margin consulting services, promising unrealistic cost savings or revenue enhancements. Their closing ratios are impressive. The phone reps, the outside reps and the business analysts make one call and then move onto the next. The company does no advertising and the pace is fast and urgent. Get an appointment. Monday, close Tuesday, do the analysis Thursday, close on consulting services Friday, deliver the services beginning Monday. It is a 100% cash business; customers pay at the end of each day. If it sounds like a well-oiled machine, well, it is. It works for a quick, one time sale, but sacrifices the long term value inherent in repeat business and exposes the firm to law suits. No customer wants to be subjected to this pressure time after time. Its values and methods may not align with yours and you wonder about the damage it does to its employees, its customers and to the image of the sales profession. Figure 1 below shows how consultive selling and the traditional "hard sell" compare on values and methods.

Feature	Consultive Selling	Traditional Selling
Values	Integrity Respect for the customer Consultive communication Sincerity	Expediency Arrogance Manipulation Deception
Competencies	Listening Probing for needs Creative problem-solving Trust-building Assertiveness Persistence	Fast-talking Probing for weaknesses Creative trickery Control Bullying, nagging, Manipulation, Pushy
Orientation	Customer needs The customer is educated to make an informed buying decision	Product promises The customer is pressured into the sale
Motivation	Service to others	Greed
Strategy	Find customer-partners Under promise, over deliver Lengthy sales cycle	Target the vulnerable Over promise, under deliver One call sale
Tactics	Build credibility and mutual respect, understand customer needs and goals, find mutually beneficial solutions and gain agreement to action plans	Impress the customer, play on fears or greed, push the product on the customer, make him take it, get the money, move onto the next qualified candidate
Measures of Success	Multiple: including customer loyalty, profit., community respect, employee satisfaction	Singular; profit.

Figure 1: Consultive versus Traditional Selling *Customer loyalty, community respect and employee satisfaction are the benefits of selecting consultive selling over a more traditional hard sell approach*

Developing an Consultive Approach to Selling

The buying process for large ticket items in most companies is complex and lengthy, increasingly requiring teams to do the buying. On the customer team there might be an *end-user,* the person who will use the product day in and day out. At some point in the buying process a purchasing manager or finance manager may get involved to assess issues such as Return-On-Investment, value, financing options and payment terms. There may be a *project manager*, responsible for ensuring that the products meet company or system-wide requirements. A *technical expert* may emerge at any point to assess the quality, reliability and performance of the product and its compatibility with other systems and tools. Job titles of these players will vary, and some people may wear more than one hat. You may have cultivated a *sponsor,* a key player in your customer's organization who is already sold on you and your solution and who has introduced you to others.

Your job is to see to it that each of these key players get answers to their questions and concerns. Make sure that you get the information you need about their requirements and needs and assess whether they are motivated to move forward through the sales process to the close. You must understand their individual and role-specific viewpoints on why their company is in the market for your products. You must develop a product/ service based solution that makes sense to their various viewpoints. You must help reconcile the sometimes competing interests they may have for purchasing your solution and be prepared to manage the anti-sponsor among them. Figure 2 below summarizes the requirements and psychological needs of each of the players on your customer's team and the recommended approach to address these needs.

Player	Business Requirements	Psychological Needs	Your Approach
Sponsor	Find a suitable business partner	Recognition	Give them the credit for a successful outcome; thank them for their confidence in you; communicate in writing and in person your appreciation for the work it took to prepare and manage the buying team. With their permission, highlight them personally in your company newsletters and customer case studies. Invite them as special guests or as speakers at company or industry events.
End-user	Ease of use Effectiveness Reliability Customer support	Respect	Provide "hands-on" opportunities for them; validate their business needs and give them the operational information they require.
Purchasing Manager	Value Terms Warranty Budget ROI Risk management	Reassurance; Purchasing Managers are often at the bottom of the totem pole and crave respect.	Prove the value of your solution with hard data. Calculate ROI. Schedule the investment installments, accrued savings and/or revenue /productivity benefits. Identify and mitigate risks. Introduce them to your senior managers.

Project Manager	Scalability Interoperability Integration Installation time-frame Support	Control	Provide installation and implementation schedules. Identify key milestones. Describe how your solution fits the big picture. Provide case studies of successful installations and customer testimonials. Provide your company's org chart, showing customer support. Introduce them to your company's senior managers. Allow them to make choices during your sales presentations. Provide product/solution options.
Technical Expert	Quality and Reliability	Recognition	Provide technical data related to quality and reliability, testimonials and case studies focusing on technical issues. Invite their questions, validate their concerns and issues and link them to experts on your sales team.

Figure 2: Strategies for five kinds of buyers *Your sales strategy must take into account the business and psychological needs of decision makers and those who influence them.*

You must first view the world from your customer's chair before presenting your solution. While it is "politically correct" to profess a customer focus, many of us are really seller focused. Though you might see the similarities among different customer's issues, customers tend to view themselves, their issues and their company as unique and may mistrust and even resent you if you characterize their issues as typical and fail to acknowledge their uniqueness.

Your customers are motivated by *pleasure,* the objectives that they are trying to achieve, or by *pain*, the worry items that keep them awake at night. For example, a sales director might anticipate with repressed excitement a job promotion that may result from opening up a new market for his products while the owner of a retail store whose sales have dramatically dropped off may be losing sleep at night. The pleasure motivator demands fulfillment while the pain cries out for relief. Pleasure and pain motivators may relate to business or psychological issues. (Motivators are also known as "needs", "hot buttons", "objectives" or "drivers". This book will simply refer to them as "needs".) Customer business needs may be to improve profits, increase sales, reduce costs, improve safety, reduce risk or improve quality. Psychological needs may be to feel in control, attain a certain status, gain prestige or simply to experience the thrill of the win.

To determine customer needs you must listen and probe deeply. For example, a plant manager may be obsessed with quality, while a CEO may be occupied with building a legacy to leave behind after he/she retires. Probe and you will find that there is always an event that precipitated the need. A competitor's poor quality control may have lead to the previous plant manager's demise. Perhaps the CEO was overlooked for an industry award, or wants to join a prestigious board after retirement.

Your customer has two to five business and/or psychological needs which are the most pressing. It's your job to get your customer to verbalize these needs, and prioritize them, so that you can analyze them and address them in your solution. In so doing you should use your customers' words to describe their needs and you should represent them accurately, resisting the temptation to exaggerate or distort them. Anything less will be perceived as manipulative and inauthentic and jeopardize any trust you have established with your customer.

Your customer may also have *wants,* which often look and sound like needs but turn out to be unnecessary for a sale. Your customer may express interest in additional services you provide, for example. At first you may be tempted to uncritically add them to the outline of a solution taking shape in your mind. As the conversation with your customer continues and deepens, your customer's and your understanding of their wants and needs become clearer. Through listening, probing and gently challenging your customer, the wants fall away leaving the needs exposed and your relationship with your customer strengthened.

Giving Customers What They Want

Sometimes you must give your customer what they want, and not what they need. Do this only when the customer's wants are not counter to their needs. Eventually your customer will come back to you for a solution that satisfies their needs. By giving them what they want you are telling your customer that you support their right and desire to make their own decision. On the other hand, if you agree to satisfy wants that you know will do serious damage to their business or psychological needs, be prepared for no follow on business. Customers often prescribe what they believe to be the solution, rather than describing for you the problem they wish to solve. Make the decision to give them what they want only after you have discovered the real problem behind the want, after you have confirmed that your customer knows that you understand the problem and after you have offered an appropriate solution. This tactic will mitigate the risk that your customer will blame you when their solution fails to solve the problem. When this happens, you can offer the solution that you have already determined will satisfy or exceed their needs. For example, your customer's want might be for your latest software, which can generate a wide variety of reports. After listening and probing customer employees you discover that employees and management disagree on which reports are critical for the business. Software that offers more reports will not solve the problem. You bring your discovery to your customer, offering to bring in a consultant to help resolve the disagreement before your customer determines which version of your software to order. Perhaps embarrassed that they did not discover the problem themselves, your customer insists on ordering what they wanted in the first place. You oblige, satisfied that your customer knows that you support them, and that the door is left open for your return.

In many cases, your customer's business requirements will be the most important driver in the buying decision. Even if the decision is based primarily on emotion (e.g., your customer loves your high-tech gadgets), the decision typically has to be justified or rationalized with a business case that will withstand inspection by other executives.

Your customer develops business requirements and determines how they will assess your solution. The acronym SPACED - Safety, Performance, Assurance, Customer service, Efficiency and Delivery - describes typical categories of requirements. Your customer formulates questions similar to those below to determine the value of your solution. Your proposal and presentation should address these questions, and in some instances, you should probe in advance to find out or clarify the level of performance your customer wants for each category. For example you might ask your customer about their delivery timetable, or about their quality standards and how they will measure them.

- **S**afety—how safe is the solution? What is the potential for failure? What are the side effects of the solution? Will the solution create more or tougher problems than it solves?

- **P**erformance—does the solution work, will it solve the problem in the way your customer has prescribed or the way you have claimed?

- **A**ssurance—does the solution meet the quality standards specified by your customer for such things as performance, appearance, form, fit, functionality, reliability and speed?

- **C**ustomer service—will you stand behind the solution? What are the service promises and how well will you meet them?

- Efficiency—are the alleged benefits derived from the solution worth the cost? Are there hidden costs or potential adverse impacts that may occur?

- Delivery—will the installation of the solution fit in the necessary time window? Will the major milestones be met? How will installation or operation of the solution affect the day-to-day operations?

Remember also to ask your customer to prioritize their requirements in order of importance, and if necessary, to explain their rationale for their rankings. Few ranking lists will be alike and the order might vary for the same customer in a different set of circumstances. How your customer prioritizes SPACED issues may be influenced by the industry in which your customer competes. Learn as much as you can before the first sales interview about how your customer does business and seize every opportunity to expand your knowledge. Explore and clarify where the customer stands on these business issues. Keep in mind too, that priorities may change or issues may come to light further down the path of the buying process.

Understanding Hidden Business Needs

Important business needs are often hidden. Some business needs, because of their sensitive nature, are not always apparent or readily shared by customers. Sometimes customers will inadvertently indicate through body language that they are not telling you everything. You must be ready to probe their body language and use follow up probes to get the full story, because these needs may have a powerful effect on your selection of a solution. Sensitive business issues may include company or division marketing strategy, business goals and confidential projects. Customers may perceive some issues as "dirty laundry". For example corporate politics, conflicting priorities, financial health, unethical practices, incompetent managers, cozy relationships with incumbent suppliers and dysfunctional corporate culture may be challenging to uncover but you must probe skillfully and persistently. The fact that you are prepared to ask questions around key business issues works in your favor. Customers will be impressed with the thoroughness of your analysis and will often learn about issues they hadn't even considered.

When customers think that their business requirements and/ or psychological needs might not be met, they may express their concerns directly to you and suggest that you work with them to analyze and solve the problem. Others may become controlling, demanding, insecure, anxious, angry, evasive, mistrustful, impatient or manipulative and may look for a convenient figure- namely you - to blame for the problem. An excessive drive for power, privilege and prestige can also produce these dysfunctional behaviors in your customers. Respond to them with empathy, insight, assertiveness and prudence. Chapter 8, Managing Customer Objections, describes techniques and methods for doing this.

How Your Customer Manages Supplier Relationships

As the downsizing and outsourcing of the current economic climate continue, customers are adopting systems and processes to manage the increasing number and variety of suppliers. One such system categorizes suppliers according to five levels of the relationship. The highest level is Partner, followed by Problem-Solver, Preferred Supplier, Qualified Supplier and Bidder. Here's how the system works.

At first you are simply another *Bidder* to them. They have not done business with you and they don't know you. They don't know what you sell, how long you have been in business, who your customers are or what you have done for them. When they get to know you they may give you a small order to see how you do with it. If you meet their standards of quality service and price, then they see you as a *Supplier*. They may then invite you to compete for more orders. If you are successful in winning more business and if you replicate your earlier success a number of times, you may become a *Preferred Supplier*. If you continue to provide value, and demonstrate increasing knowledge of your customers' business, your customers may take you into their confidence and ask you to solve problems for them without subjecting you to a competitive process. At this point your customer is elevating you to the special role of *Problem-Solver*. Finally, if you perform the problem-solver role exceptionally well by demonstrating innovation and value, and building trusting relationships at every level of your customers' organization, your customer may invite you to the status of *Partner*. At this level, your customer regards you as an "ad hoc" member of their team. They invite you to work with them to identify problems and opportunities and even to help them evaluate competitors' new products. They collaborate with your company in designing, testing and implementing solutions. They recommend you to other divisions in the organization. They adjust their organizational structure as much as you adjust yours in order to leverage opportunities. They explore joint ventures, mergers or acquisitions to leverage the relationship.

Partnership is the Goal, or is it?

Your ultimate goal in sales is to create a portfolio of profitable customers who are intensely loyal to you and who regularly send you referrals. Not every account will be a partner, nor should partnership be your goal for every account. In most sales portfolios, no more than one in 10 accounts is a true partner. Some accounts want a reliable, high-value and ongoing supply of product from a preferred supplier. Others may view your product as a commodity and seek the lowest price through frequent, competitive bidding. In these "bid and buy" situations, the product is seen as a commodity; selling is by-passed because your customer is interested only in negotiating the best price. It's like ten-pin bowling with a curtain in front of the pins. You give it your best shot and hope. When you are a supplier or a preferred supplier, the pressure is always on to demonstrate value and to keep the competition out.

You may decide to retain these customers by trading off high profit for high revenue or quality for price after assessing the partnership potential of each account. Figure 3 below shows the results of various approaches to your account list.

If Your Approach is to	Your Customer Will See You As a	Resulting in
Identify/solve problems, create opportunities	Partner	High revenue, high profit
Respond to customer-identified problems	Problem Solver	High revenue, moderate profit
Perform well repeatedly	Preferred Supplier	Moderate revenue, moderate profit
Quote and hope	Supplier	Low revenue, low profit
Bid and buy	Bidder	Low revenue, low profit

Figure 3: Step Up to Partner. *Attain the financial rewards you want by changing your sales approach*

To retain partnership status with your customer you must invest considerable time and effort in nurturing the relationship and learning about the opportunities and challenges your partner faces. Deepen insights, improve value and identify collaborative opportunities through scrutinizing their value chain, visiting other players in the industry, attending trade shows or sponsoring customer's end-user research. Work your side of the organization as well. Engage the support of senior executives in your company to commit resources, clear away any organizational barriers to collaboration and provide coaching for you when you need it.

CHAPTER 3:
RECRUITING NEW
CUSTOMERS

If you're not enthusiastic about your value proposition, how can you expect your customer to be?

From your perspective the sales cycle consists of recruiting, qualifying, fact and feeling finding, preparing and presenting a proposal, overcoming objections and closing. You, the sales rep, are the owner of the process and it is your responsibility to manage it to produce sales efficiently. However this is not your customer's view of the process. For starters, your customers call it a "buying" not a "selling" process and see themselves as the owner, managing objectives and activities to select the best supplier. The stages in the buying process are developing the specifications for the product/service solution and the criteria for selecting a supplier, confirming the budget, assessing the capabilities of suppliers, distributing a formal or informal request for proposal (RFP) to qualified suppliers, selecting finalists from proposals and inviting them to make a presentation with a question-and-answer session, and finally selecting a winner. Figure 4 below illustrates and compares the processes.

Buying Process	Selling Process
Developing specs	Recruiting candidates
Qualifying suppliers	Qualifying candidates
Distributing RFP to qualified suppliers	Information Gathering
Inviting finalists to make a presentation	Preparing and delivering a proposal
Question-and-answer session	Overcoming objections
Selecting a winner.	Closing

Figure 4: The Buying/Selling Processes Mirror Each Other.
Respect your customers' desire to manage their sales process by suggesting limited choices for next steps

The buying processes for the most part mirrors the sales cycle. The major difference is that you and your customer both feel that you ought to be in charge of the process. This means that you must take great care to respect your customers' wishes to make decisions along the way. This does not mean that you handover control. At decision points, you should summarize where you both are, ask if your customer is ready to move forward to the next stage and then suggest what that might be. Don't dictate next steps to your customer, nor passively allow your customer to tell you what to do.

Example:

You: "Before we move on, is there anything else you think I should know about the budget, Ms. Customer?"

Customer: "No, I think you have it all. As I mentioned earlier, price is important of course but we are particularly looking for a supplier who is adjustable and committed to our success, not just their own."

You: "Understood. Well then at this point, Ms. Customer, I believe I have all the information I need to develop a proposal that will knock your socks off. I'll need about three weeks to prepare it. How does that fit with your timetable?"

Customer: "You can have three weeks but if you can get it to me sooner I would appreciate it."

You: "How about this. I'll get you the electronic version in two and a half weeks, and the four bound copies you requested by the end of the third week."

Customer: "Yes, do that and have them delivered to my admin assistant by 5 PM on the Friday."

Another sticking point might occur when your customer wants to talk to your competitors and you want to go straight to a presentation and close. If you have influenced the development of the specs so that you are the best or even the only supplier qualified to deliver, your customer may decide to skip this step. That should always be your goal. However, you can still manage your sales process by treating your customer's desire to talk to competitors as an objection. Be prepared to share examples of other customers inviting suppliers to compete to comply with company policy while intending to award the business to you, the best qualified company. Lock down an early date to deliver your presentation, thus pressuring competitors to produce a proposal within a tight timeframe.

Think about the beginning of the sales process as a search for a partner to do business with. Instead of "suspects" and "prospects", substitute "candidates". Instead of a "sales call", conduct "interviews" and "meetings". This reduces the pressure to qualify and close every candidate and improves the results of your qualifying process.

Customer Recruiting is the first step in your sales process, and no matter how good a sales person you are, this is a step that you cannot skip for any significant length of time. Customer recruiting is the process of identifying and attracting candidates for your value proposition. A *candidate* is someone who appears to fit your target market, for example, a retail business with less than $5 million a year in volume in the 14607 zip code, or that shows some interest in you, your products or your company. When you find a candidate, you should immediately attempt to see if they qualify for your value proposition. You may be able to partially qualify a candidate over the telephone or by email and then secure an appointment to fully qualify them. A *qualified candidate* is someone who has the Money, the Authority and the Desire (MAD) to buy your products.

A *Customer* is someone who buys from you – once. A *Friend* is someone who buys from you more than once. And an *Advocate* is a customer who buys repeatedly from you and sends you referrals. And referrals are your best source of new business.

Generating Leads

The process of converting candidates to qualified candidates, qualified candidates to customers, customers to friends and friends to advocates is called *the sales pipeline, sales cycle or sales funnel.* Candidates may enter the sales process as a result of *lead generation* programs. Lead generation programs are marketing tactics designed to attract candidates to your company's offerings. Typical lead generation programs include direct mail, opt-in email, trade shows, advertising, web site hits, showcase events and telemarketing. Other sources of sales leads are public relations, referrals and cold calling. Rarely will you have just one or two sources of leads. The best customer recruiting programs always have referrals as the centerpiece. You are much more likely to convert a referral candidate than a cold call candidate. Most sales people dislike cold calling for good reason. It is the least efficient and most expensive method of generating candidates. Your valuable time is best invested on the phone with or in front of qualified candidates, not cold calling candidates. You may have to make as many as 100 calls to find a candidate you can covert to a qualified candidate. Lead generation programs can do this much more efficiently and cost-effectively. Leave cold-calling to the professional telemarketers, who do it better anyway. To grow your business, you must experiment with all these sources of leads to find the combination that works best for you.

View customer recruiting as an integral part of your sales pipeline. Recruiting is not something you do when you have time, or something that you rely on others to do, but is the first step in your sales process. Accept that you have to turn over a lot of rocks to find the goodies, and just take one candidate at a time. Whether it is by geography, vertical market or sales volume you should have a customer recruiting system. Organizing your customer recruiting will prevent some of the good qualified candidates from falling between the gaps and will give you a sense of accomplishment in having covered a specific market segment. Schedule customer recruiting as a routine activity you do, not monthly, or weekly, but daily. If you want a steady supply of qualified candidates, you must have a steady supply of leads.

Make friends with marketing. It's their job to generate leads. Get to know them, give them ideas and find out who they are targeting and when. If you can help them improve their results you both benefit. But do not rely exclusively on marketing, advertising or your web site, or call-ins for leads. None of them will be as productive as the ones you generate yourself by asking your customers for referrals. Call all your current and inactive clients and ask them for the names of three people who might benefit from your solutions. (You have a better chance of getting a referral if you ask for more than one). Then ask if they would be willing to phone or email the referral to prepare them for your call or, better still, invite them to lunch with you and your referrer.

If you or someone in your company is making a presentation at an industry conference, make sure that marketing does a pre-conference mailing to all conference registrants, asking them to come to your presentation or visit with you during the conference. A simple postcard followed up with a phone or email/fax blitz should do it. The important thing is that you ask your qualified candidates to commit to some action at the conference. At the conference capture details all the leads and begin to build relationships with them. You should schedule follow up phone calls with them after the conference. If they are really hot leads, schedule a meeting with them during the conference.

Create a customer recruiting plan in a simple spreadsheet, or in a more sophisticated customer relationship management or contacts management program. Your plan must include specific sales objectives, measures of success, a timetable, resources you will require, obstacles you might encounter and how you will deal with them. Your plan should also classify qualified candidates according to their strategic value or profit potential.

Segment your accounts by grouping them according to similar business criteria. Traditional segments include geography, industry or size. Segmenting them by geography can save you travel time. Segmenting them according to their industry means that you can tailor your *value proposition* to industry issues while segmenting them by revenue helps ensure you get the best value from your sales activities. If you choose to segment by geography, your value proposition will probably be fairly generic. Value propositions establish the value basis for the business relationship. They describe how your solution will improve your qualified candidate's business and how that improvement will be measured. If you segment by industry however, your value proposition can become specific about how the value will be measured. For example, a value proposition for the health care industry might include dramatic measures of the number of lives saved.

Setting goals triggers the self fulfilling prophecy phenomenon. You are more likely to be successful if you set sales goals, than if you have vague daydreams of making a lot of sales. Be careful of "analysis paralysis", the condition in which you spend too much time perfecting and analyzing your plan. However, do get into the habit of consulting your plan and updating it regularly. If not, you may easily be tempted to pursue qualified candidates that are difficult to convert to customers, or if they do become customers, are not profitable.

Increase your customer recruiting efforts not out of fear, not in a panicky, impulsive flurry of phone calls, but in a confident, methodical way. Your goal is to find customers who are buying, which means not wasting time with those who are indifferent or not ready. You must ruthlessly and rigorously qualify your candidates. Pursue only those fully qualified, not those that you think might be qualified, or those that you wish were qualified, or used to be qualified, or partly qualified, or hope they are qualified, or give the impression they are qualified, or who themselves would like to be qualified. If you are not rigorous about qualifying candidates, your mind becomes the enemy.

Creating a Sense of Urgency

Begin to create a sense of urgency as you qualify a candidate. Momentum and a sense of urgency are necessary conditions for closing sales, and it starts with your first contact with your qualified candidate. Every conversation, voice-mail, piece of literature should move your candidate to some action, no matter how small. The best way to do this is to offer plenty of benefits. For example,

1. "Mr. /Ms Qualified Candidate, we have a new/ updated/revolutionary/ breakthrough/ unique/ (creates urgency) idea/program/concept/solution/ system (never "a product") that will save you money/make you money/improve productivity. (Benefit) I'm offering you an opportunity today to evaluate/see for yourself/judge for yourself/ determine (you are in control, Ms. Qualified Candidate.) whether or not it will be of benefit and value to you. (Again, answers the question "What's In It For Me?") Our senior account exec/ director of sales/customer relationship manager (never a "sales rep"; this is much too important) will be in their area tomorrow (not a week from Friday. This is urgent!) Are you in at 7 AM or 8 AM tomorrow?" (Not "when will you be available?" Stress urgency again).

2. "Good morning/afternoon Mr. /Ms. Inactive Account. This is Sam Slick at Interpersonal Development. Do you have a couple of minutes? I thought of you recently while I was meeting with our product development people. They have come up with a very intriguing new system/model. They have figured out how to (insert a customer industry problem here _____) and apply it to your (insert typical customer business needs

here _____). My customers' end-users love the model/system, because it is so easy to use, managers love it because it leads directly to improved performance, and their finance people are delighted with it because it is so cost effective! I think it would be well worth a few minutes of your time to judge for yourself. Are mornings or afternoons best for you?" Or, "What time do you start tomorrow morning?"

3.   "Good morning, Mr. /Ms. Inactive Account this is Sam Slick at Interpersonal Development. Do you have a couple of minutes? Last time you and I spoke you talked about the challenge of (insert business issue here_____). I have just heard about an entirely new approach to this issue; in fact, I am very excited about it. The people who created this approach have already applied it to key _____ challenges of a number of your competitors. I'm sure that we have here a fresh and highly effective approach to resolving the (insert customer business issue here _____). I think we have some real benefit and value to offer, and I wanted to give you the opportunity to evaluate it for yourself. I have some holes in my schedule this week. What does first thing tomorrow look like for you?"

Door-Openers

Referrals should be one of your prime sources of new business. At the end of each call, ask if your sales contact knows of anyone else who would be interested in your product – regardless of whether or not you've closed the sale. This referral can be an effective door opener. Get ideas for door-openers by reading the business pages, the trade publications, talk to colleagues and other people in the firm you're contacting. Here are some you might try.

The *Endorsement* approach: Nothing works like a referral from a friend, colleague, or even a competitor.

> You: "Good morning, Ms. Qualified Candidate. This is Edgar Earnest of Universal Systems. One of your associates, Brenda Beeline, suggested that you might be interested in some ideas to manage your inventory."

The *Limited Opportunity* approach: A deadline, limited offers, once-in-a-lifetime opportunity presents a strong motivator.

> You: "Hello, Ms. Qualified Candidate, this is Sally Superstar of American Software. We're running a special sale on software upgrades that I know you'll want to take advantage of. The sale ends at 5 o'clock this afternoon."

The *Special Fact* approach: News about your customer's business is attention getting.

> You: "Good morning, Mr. Qualified Candidate. This is Eric Expediter of On Time Limousine Service. I just received the results of a limousine usage study of companies like yours."

The *Special Offer* approach

> You: "This month, you'll get an additional six-month service warranty free." Or, "If you order a 12-month supply, we'll defer billing for 60 days."

The *Survey* approach

You: "Your industry's association reported that
                    almost 61 percent of the companies surveyed
                    had problems with over-inventory. What is
                    your experience?"

Using Sales Scripts

In pulling together your sales message, you'll want to
choose between a script and a prompt guide. Use a
script when your message must be concise, your service
or product is complex, your customer is unfamiliar
with your product, you are inexperienced at telesales, or
when legal issues could be involved. Call early morning.
Leaving your sales message on voice mail is like a free
advertisement for you and your company. Call again late
afternoon. If you are not able to connect, leave your sales
pitch on voice mail again, adding that you will call again
later. Don't ask the qualified candidate to return your call
- they won't. Don't even leave your phone number – that's
just wishful thinking. If you tell them you will call again
and then leave your phone number you are giving them a
mixed message, which is not a good way to start a business
relationship.

First Contact Example

You: "My name is Rhonda Restless, Account
                    Executive at Growth Unlimited, LLC, and
                    I'm calling to introduce myself. Do you have
                    a few minutes?"

Candidate: "Just half of one, actually. What is this
                    about?"

You:

"My firm has helped one of your competitors, Corporate Research Associates, achieve some pretty significant results through our unique business development programs. I'd like to offer you the opportunity to see if my company can benefit you the same way. How does your schedule look next Monday at 2 PM?"

OR "Our programs have been very successful with a number of companies in your industry; I thought you would like to know about it."

Persistence Example

You:

"Hello Mr. Candidate, this is Susan Seller with ABC.com I'm calling to follow up on your recent email concerning our business development programs."

Candidate:

"I vaguely remember you; frankly, I requested info from several business development companies."

You:

"Why don't we get together and I'll share with you some of the unique opportunities we have created. How's your schedule look later this week?"

Candidate:

"Well, I'm only exploring what's out there just now. Call me again in three weeks or so."

You:

"I can certainly do that. It sounds like a really good overview of the business development industry might help you sort out what you are looking for and help you with your planning. I have a presentation that does just that. Would you want to consider taking a look at that now?"

Candidate: "That might be useful… call me next week and we will set something up."

You: "Can we pencil it in now, and I'll call to confirm next week?"

Candidate: "OK"

Enter results in your contact management software program and continue calling each day until contact is made. Persistence counts. According to a recent National Sales Executive Association survey, 80 percent of all new sales are made at the fifth call to the same qualified candidate. If you fail to connect on the fifth call, leave your sales message again, express your regret that you have not been able to make contact, state that you will not call again, and this time leave your phone number with a request for a call-back. Then file the candidate for a six- month follow up and move on to the next candidate.

Developing Your Elevator Pitch

Follow up your door opener with an *elevator pitch*. So called because it should take no more than the time it takes an elevator to get to the ground floor. Your elevator pitch delivers your company's overall value proposition to its target markets and should include who you are, what you do for whom and why you are the best choice. It should be your memorized response to the question, "What do you do?" Your elevator pitch should be easy to remember and easy to say. Keep it simple and free of jargon. You want to engage the listener, so make it as interesting as possible. As you write your elevator pitch, say it out loud. Time it and test it on people to see what flows.

Example

> You:
>
> "Interpersonal Development helps organizations experiencing product, market or cultural change win more business. We offer consulting in sales, marketing and leadership development. Our customized process combines Behavioral Modeling Technology™ with an interactive climate that is supportive, nonjudgmental and engaging.
>
> The result is that your team feels understood, valued and motivated to perform for you. Everybody wins. Your colleagues are impressed, your competitors stunned and your customers delighted".

Your *sales pitch* is longer than your elevator pitch and explains your value proposition and key benefits. It should convey an understanding of your qualified candidate's pain and how your product/service can solve it. There's more on the sales pitch in Chapter 7: Preparing and Presenting your Proposal.

Cold Calling

Cold calling is the process of approaching candidates, typically via telephone, who have not agreed to such an interaction. The word "cold" is used because the person receiving the call is not expecting the call or has not specifically asked you to contact them. It is often very frustrating and difficult because candidates often rebuff, hang-up and reject you.

Cold calling that enables you to call without being rejected is based on the idea that the purpose of the call is not to make a sale, but to build trust and discover the truth about whether there is a good match between the candidate and your product or service. Start with a high quality, up-to-date database consisting of candidates that have demonstrated an interest in your products or services. Rather than using the call to try to close a sale, think of it as the initial contact in a long-term relationship. This has the effect of removing the sales pressure from calls and making the goal of your call to build trust. You can also use cold calls to obtain quality sales leads, references, and testimonials. Make cold calling in person a routine best practice by dropping in on the business establishment to either side of the one where you have an appointment. Say to the receptionist, "I'd like to leave my business card for Mr. Candidate. Would you do me a favor and see that he gets it? And by the way, may I have his/her business card?"

When on the telephone with your customers take care to enunciate clearly. The telephone exaggerates slurring or mispronunciation of words. Hold the phone about a half-inch from your mouth and don't use a speakerphone for sales interviews. Sit up straight in your chair and monitor your use of your voice by using a mirror to ensure your facial expressions are aligned with your verbal messages. Make most of your calls in the morning when your voice is rested.

Qualified Recruiting by the Numbers

For most industries, there are some rough ratios to work with. To get one sale, you should solicit requests to submit three proposals. To submit three proposals you should be talking to three to six qualified candidates. To find five or six qualified candidates you probably should screen at least 100 candidates. Sorting out candidates and qualified candidates is what direct mail, trade shows, advertising and telesales do best. You should be spending most of your time with qualified candidates, not playing telephone tag with unqualified candidates.

Stay in touch with qualified candidates over a long sales cycle through web conferences that update customers on product changes, certification issues, pricing changes or promotions. Schedule regular web events for training, or question and answer sessions and online demos conducted by your internal product experts.

There is a build up to a successful close. Rarely does the customer make a quick, impulsive decision. Usually the sales process starts slowly and gathers momentum. Near the end, the momentum takes over, so that the customer gets driven inevitably towards the close. Along with momentum comes a sense of urgency. Closing the deal becomes a priority for the customer. Get your customers talking about the market and ask them how it is affecting their business, their department, their job, and listen for the pain. Show them how your product or service reduces it. Sell them peace of mind. Sell them hope, there is light at the end of the tunnel, if you buy my product. Sell yourself as an ally in the competitive game they are in.

Setting Call Objectives

Before every sales interview, on the telephone or in the field, you should do some background research on your qualified candidate or customer, prepare call objectives, questions, sales aids, coach of any technical experts or other team members, ideas or proposals to present and expected sales call outcomes. Pre-call planning also may involve phone conversations with key players inside the customer organization.

To prepare for each call, begin by setting call objectives. Overall objectives may be to create interest in your product, build your customer profile, overcome objections, and if appropriate, close the sale. Depending on the type of call and the product you're selling, your call objectives would be more specific. Ask yourself why you are calling that account. Depending on the type of call and the type of business you represent, your call objective might be to qualify candidates, build a customer profile, make initial contacts or identify the decision-maker, announce special sales or discounts, provide new product information, follow up on past orders, head off the competition, obtain testimonial or handle complaints.

Your sales message should incorporate phrases that will intrigue and hold your customer's attention. Train yourself to listen attentively to your customer and to probe your customer's message. Expect and formulate responses to objections that you are likely to hear about your product or company, anticipate the ways in which your product or service will meet the needs of your customer, and plan to up-sell and cross-sell.

You will get objections to closing on the appointment. Here are a few:

Example 1

Customer: "Send me some information first".

You: "I can do one better than that. One of our product developers, Karen Creator, will be in Phoenix tomorrow, so she can walk you through the information personally. Will you be in around 3:30 PM?"

Example 2

Customer: "Now is a bad time."

You: "I certainly appreciate how valuable your time is Mr. Inactive Account. However, it will only take you five minutes to see if we have anything of benefit or value for you. What would be easiest, tomorrow morning or afternoon?"

Example 3

Customer: "We had record sales last year. We don't need your _____."

You: "That is exactly why I called you. Some of our best customers are exceptionally successful, and in part, it is because they are continuously raising the bar. They take advantage of new ideas to make the small changes that keep them just that much better than the competition. You will know in the first five minutes if we can improve your operation. How's tomorrow, first thing?"

Example 4

Customer: "Have no budget"

You: "I met with a (insert candidate's industry here) company recently. They had some pretty good plans in place already, and what budget they had was fully allocated. Because they like to keep abreast of the industry, they agreed to meet us for just a few minutes. The manager was so impressed with what he heard that he immediately scheduled a meeting for us with some key colleagues. No commitments of course, but clearly there was a company that could see real value in exploring fresh ideas."

Example 5

Customer: "Give me some more info first."

You: "What would you like to know?"

Customer: "Well, what is this model/system, has it been applied to our industry, what kind of ROI is it getting? I've got a million questions."

You: "I'd be happy to explain to you on the phone but I'm not sure I could do justice to the power of the system/model. I guarantee you'll be impressed with it within the first few minutes of our meeting. Tomorrow, late morning, or early afternoon?"

Qualifying Candidates – Are They MAD?

A critical objective in qualified Recruiting is qualifying, which determines if a person who has shown some interest in your value proposition has the potential to become a customer. *Candidates* therefore, are potential buyers who have not yet been qualified. The general criteria for qualifying are neatly summarized by the acronym MAD; does your candidate have the Money, the Authority and the Desire. Your candidate must meet all three criteria to qualify as a qualified candidate. A *qualified candidate* is a potential customer who has met the qualifying criteria but has not yet made a purchase. A *customer* is a qualified candidate who has paid for your product or service. (Some say a qualified candidate is not a customer until the check has been cashed.)

Time invested in listening for needs, preparing and presenting a proposal can be completely wasted if your candidate is not qualified (for example, has no budget). A candidate who is not the decision-maker may, for ego reasons, act as if he is. Ask probing questions about the decision making process to determine your candidate's role and responsibilities. Similarly, don't be seduced by the opportunity to talk to a decision-maker with a big budget, who "should" be interested in your offerings. The excitement of such an opportunity can cloud your judgment, and lead you to deny the reality, gloss over the facts or assume that your candidate is fully qualified. But if you cannot stir some emotion in candidates, or convince them that you have something of value to offer, they will remain unqualified. Your attempts to move ahead and "sell" your candidate on requesting a proposal are usually a waste of your time.

In addition to the time spent, there are always hard costs involved in working a candidate through the sales cycle. Preparing and presenting a proposal can entail substantial costs of employee time, presentation materials, and travel expenses. Companies that measure and track their cost of sales quickly realize that they can lower their cost simply by improving the effectiveness of their qualifying.

Inadequate qualifying may also take its toll on your morale. While sales wins are enormously motivating, too many sales losses can discourage sales activity. When you are discouraged you tend to blame forces outside your control, like the market, the product, the territory, etc. This downward cycle can be prevented by good qualifying. With a well qualified candidate, the chances of a win are significantly better, and your morale will remain high.

As the trend towards team-based organization structures and outsourcing to preferred partners continues, qualifying your candidate becomes more complex. The person who makes the final choice of a supplier may not be the person who controls the budget, or even the person who stands most to benefit from the solution. In this instance, identify the role each person plays, make sure you understand the steps in the decision making and budgeting processes, and then qualify the organization.

For example, assume that your imaging software helps fire departments locate the nearest fire hydrant during a fire. The local fire chief might be enthusiastic about your product, but it might be the mayor who decides whether or not to buy the software and the finance director who controls the budget. The fire chief is a candidate. If you can get the fire chief, the mayor, and the finance director together, you might be able to qualify the group as a qualified candidate. However, if the finance director can't or won't provide the funds, this group isn't qualified. Move on to the next municipality.

Your qualifying objective is to determine your candidate's level of interest in your company's capabilities or value proposition. Sometimes it is evident, other times you must do some digging. You must also reverse the order of our MAD acronym. It may be important to you to find out first if they have the money, but you are more likely to gain their confidence and cooperation if you begin with Desire. Begin with easy to answer probes concerning the Desire issues, saving the most sensitive Money issues to last, when your candidate is feeling more comfortable with you. If you have a particularly sensitive question you want to ask and your candidate has been guarded in the early part of your sales call, try the Colombo technique. End the sales call, stand up and begin walking towards the door. Pause and as if just remembering, say, "Oh, just one last question." Catching your candidate off-guard, you might get your answer.

Remember that your candidate's Desire falls into one of two categories – pain or pleasure. Pain could be a business problem that must be solved to avert negative effects on the bottom line or your candidate's career. Pleasure could be making more money, increasing productivity or for the individual, basking in the recognition of succeeding in a high profile project. Candidates buy to relieve pain or enhance pleasure, and it is your job, when qualifying, to find the source of the pleasure or pain and empathize with your candidate.

Here are some qualifying questions for Desire.

Goals

- What are your top three business goals for this year?

- How important are these goals to your company's growth plans?

- How do they support the company's growth strategy?

- What happens to managers at your company who achieve or exceed their goals?

- What happens if you do not achieve these goals?

- How does this project fit into your business plans?

Solutions

- What are some of the solutions you have tried in the past (or currently using)?

- What results did you get?

- Were those results acceptable?

- What kinds of solutions are you considering this time?

- What results do you expect?

- What thoughts do you have about measuring results?

- (Different bullet sizes?) What other methods did you consider to achieve your goals?

- Are you open to considering some creative ideas?

Your Competition

- What other firms/suppliers are you talking to?

- Do you have a specific proposal from them?

- What is in it?

- What criteria are you going to use to select a partner?

- Which criterion is the most important to you?

- Do we have a shot at this?

Final Question

- Is there anything else you think I should know about your plans?

The next qualifying criterion is Authority, which means determining who in your candidate's organization would sign-off on your proposal. These issues may not be as sensitive as the Money issues but are more delicate than your Desire probes. There may be more than one person who signs-off on your proposal. There may be a CFO who signs-off on the funding, a Project Manager who signs-off on the selection of suppliers and a team of end-users, managers and experts who make the final selection. Only by probing can you sort out these relationships. Here are some examples of questions that probe the Authority issues.

Decision Making

- What is the decision-making process for this project?

- Who else do you need to consult before making a decision?

- Is there any one else you think I should talk to about this project?

- Whose head will roll if this project is not a success?

Last Question

- Is there anything else you think I should know about your decision-making process?

There are three parts to the Money qualification. Determine if your candidate has a budget for the project, and if not, how your candidate intends to fund it. You must also identify who in your candidate organization will authorize the expenditure. Probing is especially important here because some candidates, for reasons of pride, do not like to admit they don't have any money, or that they must go to someone higher for approval.

Here are some questions that help qualify a candidate on the Money criterion.

Budget Size

- Whose budget is this coming out of?

- How much have you set-aside for this project?

- How are you proposing to fund the project?

- Are there any other projects competing for these dollars?

Budget Process

- What is your company's process for funding these types of investments?

- When does the budget process begin?

- What are the steps in your budgeting process?

Last Question

- Is there anything else you think I should know about your budget?

To close the qualifying sales interview, first tie up any loose ends. For example, confirming names and phone numbers of other people in the account who need to be qualified. Then review any action steps that were agreed to or suggested during the call. Giving qualified candidates an assignment, no matter how small, is an effective way to keep them invested and involved in the sales process.

The result of probing is that you convert a cool, unknown candidate to a warm, qualified candidate. In large, complex sales where the customer has issued a *Request for a Proposal* (RFP), probing also helps you determine whether or not to bid at all. Good qualifying reveals if you should invest your time and energy in a qualified candidate, and for example, go to a demonstration or trial. Finally, good probing reveals your qualified candidate's buying needs, setting you up for a winning proposal.

CHAPTER 4:
LISTENING TO CUSTOMER NEEDS

Improve your listening by taking the cotton out of your ears and putting it in your mouth

There is no better way to communicate your interest in an authentic relationship with your customer than through listening to your customer's needs.

Listening to customer needs means communicating your understanding back to your customer in a way that deepens your customer's awareness and understanding of their needs and moves the sale forward. Listening allows you to identify the "must have" elements of a solution from the "nice to have", through understanding and responding to customer verbal and non-verbal ("body language") messages.

Use listening to qualify your customers, to make a bid/no bid decisions, to overcome objections and to negotiate win/win agreements. At the beginning of the sales process you listen to qualify your customer and then you listen to understand their business requirements and psychological needs. Later on, when preparing and presenting your proposal, you listen to assess the impact your solution is having on your customer. To effectively overcome objections and to negotiate terms and conditions you listen to your customers' underlying psychological needs rather than the initial position they may assume. And success in closing is more about listening for your customers' buying signals than about applying the closing technique.

Example

> Customer: "Our CEO has three key initiatives this year that involve coordinated, cross-department service delivery. We have never done that before, and we have never had such an aggressive implementation timetable. So if your company has some new, breakthrough software solution…"
>
> You: "That depends, Tom. What is your role in this initiative?"
>
> Customer: "I'm the guy the CEO appointed to make this happen. I'm heading up a cross departmental, cross-functional planning and implementation team. For me, this is a significant project."
>
> You: "How significant, Tom?"
>
> Customer: "It's a high visibility, high value project. If it's a success, I'll be a hero."

To listen effectively, you must remain detached and dispassionate about your own emotions or they'll interfere with your ability to hear what's really being said. You must develop the ability to hear exactly what's being said and to probe and clarify until the underlying message is crystal clear. Notice even a subtle change in your customer's psychological temperature. Imagine that someone who was gung-ho about your idea 10 minutes ago suddenly starts answering your questions with "Yeah, well, O.K." That drop in enthusiasm should be a warning to you to probe. For example, you might say,

"A minute ago you seemed so excited. Has something occurred to you, something that's come up in our discussion that's got you thinking in another direction?"

Never make your customers feel that they are being interrogated. Your listening and probing should feel to the customer like a thoughtful, conversation with a friend. You need a full understanding of the situation, yet your customers shouldn't feel pestered, pressed or manipulated because you're firing questions at them non-stop. That will surely make them clam up and your aim is just the opposite. You don't want the interaction to degenerate into an exchange in which your customers provide fragmented answers, or become hostile to you instead of considering your idea, product or service. Pace your customer's energy level and feeling level. The idea is to communicate that you are on his/her wavelength, in sync, in-tune with him/her. An occasional *acknowledgement* – "yes", "I see", etc. shows the customer you are listening and interested, but be careful not to overdo this technique.

Listening and Probing go Hand in Hand

But be sure to ground your questions in specifics, otherwise the qualified candidates tend to generalize and digress about what could be, should be or might be, rather than to zero in on what is. For example, you might say, "Maybe you could tell me what happened the last time you purchased a product like this. What were your objectives and what were the obstacles you encountered? What was the outcome?" This line of probing will tell you much about your customer's buying process, and what to expect this time.

Having asked your initial questions and gotten your qualified candidate talking, you'll want to keep probing and clarifying, but not in a way that stops the flow. Don't interrupt with abrupt, pointed questions. That will land you back in a verbal Ping-Pong game, where questions and answers are being batted across the net and the ball is inevitably dropped. Instead, all that is often required is to gently prompt the qualified candidate with "Go on," or "That's very interesting, tell me more."

Continuing with your sales interview with your customer, Tom:

You:	"Sounds like a wonderful opportunity, Tom, and also a lot of pressure. How will you measure success?"
Customer:	"Two ways. We've got to be able to show cost savings of x million dollars and we have to hit every milestone on our launch and delivery timetable."
You:	"And what do you anticipate will be the biggest obstacle to success?"
Customer:	"You mean besides me and my big mouth? .... I'd say getting everyone on the same page. The people on my team are all senior executives with their own high priority projects. I don't know where some of them are going to find the time for my project."
You:	"I'm beginning to see the picture. Sounds like you really have your hands full. The more I hear the more confident I am that we can offer you and your team a system and tools that will save time in coordinating the implementation. As well as project and track cost savings. Interested?"
Customer:	"Maybe. Show me how it works."

Note the listening, clarifying and probing sequence in this sales dialogue.

You: "I'm confused, Ellen. This morning you emphasized that you need adjustability. As you nicely put it, you want your technology to support people and change, not the other way around. With a fixed-price contract, your suppliers will be forced to increase their prices to cover the inflation risk, which means that you might not realize the long term cost savings you want. Are you open to alternative financing?"

Customer: "I doubt it. The cost savings are critical for us, and a fixed price contract benefits you too. This is a win-win provision."

You: "Would you be prepared to trade-off cost savings for adjustability?"

Customer: "Your proposal must address both cost savings and adjustability, while supporting people."

You: "OK , I'm trying to put myself in your shoes. I want to know that I'm paying less for the next five years than I'm currently paying. At the same time, I want a solution adjustable enough to adapt to change, while supporting people. Ellen, what do you mean by "supporting people"?

Customer: "Perhaps "supporting" is not quite the right word. Perhaps, "user-friendly technology", is a more accurate descriptor. We want the technology to adapt to change but we don't want to burden our people with unnecessary, "whistles and bells", and we don't want them to spend long periods of time in the classroom learning new applications every time a change comes along. They are stressed enough already."

You: "Right. So you will want a relationship with a partner who understands your changing needs, who can perhaps anticipate changes, who can help you manage the changes, and be especially sensitive to the impact of the changes on people. Am I on target?"

Converting candidates to qualified candidates, qualified candidates to customers, customers to friends and friends to advocates requires accurate and empathic listening and laser-like probing. You should always be listening to and observing your customer. You should be listening even when you are the one speaking. *Empathic listening* means being in tune with your customers' feelings and perceptions from moment to moment, while remaining non-judgmental and focused on your objectives. Listen for customer reactions to your words, the unspoken message expressed through body language. Listen for themes, hot buttons and points of agreement with your customer. Listen for ideas not just words – You want to get the whole picture, not just isolated bits and pieces. Listen for your customer's story. Listen for understanding and to build trust. Listen to answers to your questions, hidden objections, feedback and pathways to a to a win-win agreement.

Similarly, listen for your customer's perspective on the problem and be aware that perspectives may vary. What to you might seem to be a minor inconvenience, to a customer might represent the core issue. Your ability to take your customer's perspective communicates your authenticity, adjustability, intelligence, and your respect for your customer, which builds trust and leads to more business.

Removing Barriers to Listening

Listening has been devalued in business, which views speaking as active, and listening as passive. Dissatisfied customers will more frequently complain that you, "didn't listen" than "didn't speak well." When customers feel listened to, they feel positively disposed towards you. If you listen to them, they will tell you all that you need to know to win their business. If you listen when your customers are describing their problems and opportunities, when it comes time for you to describe your proposal they will be more likely to listen to you. When you listen, you are showing respect and caring. By listening, you communicate your desire to understand them and their business. This, in turn, increases your customers' expectations that you will return with a proposal that addresses their needs. Listening non-defensively to customer complaints and objections also communicates to customers that you are interested, concerned but not afraid. This increases their confidence that you will have an answer to their concerns.

Customers may put up barriers to listening. They mumble, don't complete sentences, express ideas poorly, use distracting mannerisms, have negative or condescending attitudes towards you, or even a hostile or intimidating demeanor. As a result you focus on the barriers instead of the message and consequently miss or distort your customer's message. Noisy surroundings, lack of privacy, telephone interruptions, not being face-to-face with the customer and a crowded or messy office are environmental barriers that may distract you. You can ask your customer to change the venue but there's not much else you can do about these barriers.

Barriers that you can do something about are those you put up yourself. Instead of focusing on your customers, you may try to impress them with how much you know. When you do the talking and your customer does the listening you learn nothing about what you must do to close the sale. You can hear and process about 600 words a minute. The average person speaks at 200 words a minute and so your mind wanders, you may become distracted and it may appear to your customer that you are not interested. You think you know exactly what your customer is going to say next and consequently hear only what you want to hear.

You may get turned off by your customer's personality, offensive remarks, or critical comments made about your company. Your hurt feelings may interfere with your ability to objectively hear your customer's message. You may become distracted by a personal problem or simply thinking about lunch. Leave your own worries in your car. Personal fears, worries, and problems that are not connected to the task of listening to a customer can blank out the customer's message. You cannot believe what you just heard because it was so completely unexpected and so your mind blocks it from memory. If you are distracted by these other factors, you may move into problem-solving mode before your customer is ready and she will get frustrated and mentally dismisses you because you don't listen. You may start giving free advice before your customer has finished describing his needs, running the risk of being perceived as a know-it-all, or a product-pusher. Don't jump to conclusions. Perhaps you feel you know exactly what he/she's going to say next. Perhaps you're right and perhaps not, but if you have stopped listening you may miss the subtle differences in what your customer actually says from what you expected them to say.

Monitor and manage your feelings to mitigate against under or over reacting to your customer. Your feelings influence your response to your customer. For example, you have a verbal commitment from your customer and now you are trying to hold the line on your pricing. It's late Friday afternoon and your customer insists on a five percent discount for no particular reason. Immediately a little voice tells you that she is not going to sign the order unless she gets her discount and that if you don't close this deal today, you won't be able to take off Monday as planned. Fear kicks in and you move into action. You hear yourself saying, "No worries, Ms. Customer, I think we can arrange that for such a good customer". Sometime later you learn that your customer's target price was in fact eight percent over the price she paid and that she had to make a decision that day because she was going on vacation the following week. The five percent discount was a bluff. In this example your feelings interfered with your judgment which leads to you taking the wrong course of action. Instead of probing her request you reacted out of fear.

Taking Notes

Many barriers to effective listening can be avoided by simply taking an active, positive role. Take notes. Immediately after a conversation, researchers say, you only retain about 55 percent of the information your customer has provided. (Two days later, that percentage drops to 25.) Taking notes selectively, however, helps preserve key points. Note taking also forces you to concentrate. Ask questions about what your customer is saying. Not only will the answers broaden your own base of knowledge, but you will also clear up any misunderstanding as they arise. Taking notes also communicates to your customers that you are listening and that you understand their unique needs. Note taking subconsciously reinforces your customer. Encourage your customer's further disclosure of information by openly taking notes, and discourage useless information by not taking notes on it. Attempts to note everything your customer says are doomed to failure and appear to your customer that you are indiscriminate and ill informed.

Paraphrasing your Customer's Message

Paraphrasing is a listening skill that you use to ensure that you have heard what your customer intended you to hear, to buy yourself time to recover from a failed tactic, to regain control of your sales interview, to interrupt a customer who is repetitive or aimless and to reassure your customer that you grasp their key message. The paraphrase is a tool that you use in every sales interview, multiple times. Paraphrasing is one of the conditions necessary to close deals. Paraphrasing means restating in your own words the essential meaning of what your customer says. It requires listening to your customer's story, paying attention to words and body language and neither subtracting nor adding content. Be careful not to subtract content that you did not like, were not expecting to hear or that made no sense to you. Guard against adding content that you wished your customer had said, or expected your customer to say or adding "missing" content that would make sense to you.

Example

You:	"Mr. Customer, you mentioned supplier problems earlier. What happened exactly?"
Customer:	"They just don't get it. They quickly respond to all our service requests, including outages and requests for upgrades, but they don't see the big picture. They have made no attempt to analyze the patterns of service complaints and email usage. They have not proposed changes at the systemic level. They are nice people, but we have outgrown them. They were shocked when I announced I was putting together a RFP."

You:	"So you are looking for a partner who can not only propose the best solution, but also one who is proactive, and can feed you ideas and alert you to issues. Am I right?"
Customer:	"You are right on, though you probably won't find it put quite so clearly in the RFP."

Listening with Empathy

Empathy is the ability to put yourself in the shoes of your customer and experience events and emotions the way they do. Since your customer's state of mind, beliefs, and desires are intertwined with their emotions, through empathy you may often be able to more effectively define your customer's mode of thought and mood. Empathy enables you to "read" your customer, translating body movements into understandable conversation that moves the sales process forward. Confronted with their aspirations and fears your customer becomes clearer about what they want while your understanding supports their attempts to articulate it. The bond that empathy forms strengthens your relationship with your customer, gives you insight into their situation and an edge over your competitors. Empathy also is a key component of authenticity in your customer relationships.

Being empathetic requires that you momentarily put aside your agenda, your thoughts and feelings, let your guard down and "put yourself in the shoes" of your customer without attempting to judge or problem-solve it. Empathy is a gift – a gift of yourself at a point in time to your customer. Research shows that women are naturally better at it than men, but men can learn to improve their empathy with their customers.

Making the effort to develop and apply your empathy will enable you and your customer to understand your customer's business and psychological needs and collaborate in developing a solution.

Example 1

Customer:	"Our current email system is nuts. For starters, we've got too many unnecessary mail boxes. Even the janitors have mail boxes! The system is painfully slow and we have had too many outages. It has limited remote access capability. Some departments have bought upgrades, their own anti-spam and anti-pop-up applications, and the entire system, if you can call it a system that runs off 37 different servers! Can you believe that! 37! We even found one server in a coat closet!"
You:	"Sounds like you are really frustrated with it. (Customer nods, eyes downcast) What have you done so far to fix it?"

Example 2

You:	"You are still not comfortable with it, are you? I can understand your reluctance. I sit in your office and tell you that we can do this project for you, I show you a letter from a customer, but those nagging doubts are still there, aren't they." (Arms still crossed, customer shrugs apologetically.)

Figure 5 below defines four levels of empathy and their effects on the outcome of your fact-gathering sales interview. Note how much more productive the Expert's sales interview is than the Novice's.

Listening and Probing Competency Levels

Level 1 (Novice)

You can get some of the facts of a situation and observe some of your customer's overt feelings about the situation.

Level 2 (Competent)

You can get some of the facts of the situation, the implications for your customer's business and its personal impact on them. You can uncover some of your customer's feelings about the key facts and can read obvious body language.

Level 3 (Proficient)

You can get most of the facts of the situation, the implications for your customer's business and its personal impact on them. You can uncover and develop customer's feelings about the key facts and read subtle body language.

Level 4 (Expert)

You can get all the facts of the situation, the implications for your customer's business and its personal impact on them. You can uncover and develop your customer's feelings about the key facts. You can read and respond to subtle body language. You can communicate your understanding back to your customer in a way that deepens your customer's awareness and understanding of their own needs.

Figure 5: Listening and probing competency levels *Use these descriptions to assess your listening and probing skills with your customers*

CHAPTER 5:
CONVERTING QUALIFIED CANDIDATES TO CUSTOMERS

"Collecting data is like collecting garbage. Pretty soon, we have to do something with it."
                                    —*Mark Twain*

When you have separated the candidates from the qualified candidates you are ready to move into the most critical part of the sales cycle, sorting candidates from qualified candidates through the qualifying process. Recall that candidates are qualified if they have the money, if they have the authority and if they have the desire to buy. When qualified candidates meet all three criteria, they are worth pursuing. The opposite of qualifying is disqualifying. If they fail to meet one or more of the criteria, you should disqualify them, and continue your search elsewhere. The odds are good that a qualified candidate might buy from you, but the odds are poor that an unqualified candidate will. Don't waste your time pursuing unqualified candidates. The quiet death of many sales can often be traced back to a failure to qualify the candidate.

Time invested in listening for needs, preparing and presenting a proposal can be completely wasted if your candidate is not qualified (for example, has no budget). Candidates who are not the decision-makers may, for ego reasons, act as if they are. Ask probing questions about the decision making process to determine your candidate's role and responsibilities. Similarly, it is easy to be seduced by the opportunity to talk to a decision-maker with a big budget, who "should" be interested in your offerings. The excitement of such an opportunity can cloud your judgment, and lead you to deny the reality, gloss over the facts or assume that your candidate is fully qualified. But if you cannot stir some emotion in your candidate, or convince your candidate that you have something of value to offer, your candidate remains unqualified, and attempts to move ahead and "sell" your candidate on requesting a proposal are usually a waste of time.

In addition to the time savings, there are always hard costs involved in converting candidates to advocates. Preparing and presenting a proposal can entail substantial costs of your time, presentation materials, and travel expenses. Companies that measure and track their cost-of-sales quickly realize that they can lower their cost simply by improving the effectiveness of their qualifying.

Inadequate qualifying also takes its toll on your morale. While sales wins are enormously motivating, too many sales loses can discourage sales activity. When you are discouraged, you may tend to blame forces outside your control, like the market, the product, or your territory. This downward cycle can be prevented by good qualifying. With a well qualified candidate, the chances of a win are significantly better, while your morale remains high.

As the trend towards team-based organization structures and outsourcing to preferred partners continues, qualifying your candidate becomes more complex. The customer who makes the final choice of a partner may not be the person who controls the budget, or even the person who stands most to benefit. In this instance, you must identify the role each person plays, the steps in the decision making and budgeting processes, and then qualify the organization.

Converting Candidates to Qualified Candidates; are they MAD?

Qualified candidates, also known as "hot prospects", are potential customers who have the *Money, Authority and Desire (MAD)* to buy from you. Having the money includes a budget for the product, source of funding, or a purchase order number. Having the authority to buy may be signified by job title or signature on previous or similar orders. Your candidate may have the authority to purchase products up to a certain dollar level, after which they must seek approval from someone else. Having the desire means that they have a problem for which your product is a solution, or an opportunity which your product can realize. Be careful that you don't mistake interest in your product for desire. Having an interest in your product is not the same as a desire. Candidates may be interested for some vague, future project, or they may be simply curious.

Until you have established that they meet all three of the MAD criteria, they are simply candidates. Candidates are potential customers who meet at least one of the MAD criteria. Some may have the authority to buy, and the budget for what you sell, but not have the desire. Some have the desire and the authority to buy, but not have the budget for what you sell. Others may have the desire, and the budget, but not have the authority to buy what you sell. Qualified candidates are those who have the desire, the budget, and the authority to buy what you sell.

Let's say your imaging software helps real estate companies locate the nearest elementary school. In a large real estate firm, the brokers and agents may be very enthusiastic about your product, but it may be the CEO that makes the decision and the finance director who controls the budget. If you can get the CEO and the finance director together, you may be able to qualify the firm as a qualified candidate. However, if the finance director cannot or will not fund it, the firm is not qualified. Invest no more time in this candidate and move on to the next.

Benefits of Qualifying

Control the sales process by qualifying candidates. Your manager may urge you to, "get out there and sell someone," "close more sales," or "move product." These are critical objectives which can only be accomplished by first determining if there is an opportunity to do business. Asking qualifying questions allows you, not your candidates, to control the agenda. Your candidates may approach you wanting to know your product specs and pricing. If you respond with this information, you lose control of the sales process. Your candidates may end the process right there, because they do not understand how your products can solve their problems. Asking questions gives you control. Answering questions loses control.

Save time and money by qualifying. Qualifying a candidate must be your very first objective. If you put it off, and instead make impressive sales presentations or prepare lengthy proposals, you may be wasting your time. In the real estate firm above, the managing broker may invite you to make presentations to all her managers. She may invite you to prepare a detailed proposal. She may even set up a meeting for you to deliver your presentation and proposal to the CEO. You could spend weeks going through this process, generating high interest and getting lots of encouragement from everyone you meet. You could rearrange your sales priorities, you could plan how you will spend your sales commission, and you could promise your sales manager that it is a "slam dunk". And then one day, weeks later, you find out that the finance director has killed it. All that time, energy and resources are wasted, and all your hopes are dashed. You are left feeling frustrated and discouraged. You calculate how many other sales you might have closed if you had only qualified the finance director. And your sales manager calculates the financial cost of all those futile sales presentations.

Qualifying makes your job easier. When you qualify a candidate, you are simplifying and focusing your sales efforts. Qualifying is an objective test of reality for you. It tempers your enthusiasm, it focuses your activity, and it channels your energy. Applying the qualifying criteria prevents emotion from interfering with good business sense. It helps us separate the "should be", "could be" and "might be" candidates from the qualified candidates. It also puts a check on the hoped for, the wished for and the, "probably are", games our minds tend to play.

Qualifying paves the way for partners. When you qualify candidates you communicate to them that you are a professional who values his/her time and who values your candidates' too. You are also suggesting that you are seeking partners, not pushing products. Your solution is not for everyone. Only a privileged few may benefit from your exclusive opportunity. Qualifying is then perceived by your candidates as more like a selection interview than a sales presentation. Your objective is to get your candidates to hope that they will qualify and be selected. Furthermore, when you are qualifying candidates, you are essentially listening to them as they talk about their favorite topic - themselves. When you listen to candidates you are creating an implied agreement. When it is your turn to talk, they feel obliged to listen.

Probing is the Key Skill

The main skill you need for qualifying is the probe. *Probing* means digging below the surface and uncovering unspoken needs. Skillful probing actually enables you to direct and control your sales interview by eliciting information as you need it. Use *open ended probes* to gather information. Open probes cannot be answered with a "yes" or "no".

They encourage your customer to open up and give you the information you are seeking. Open probes begin with who, what, when, where, why and how. Be especially careful when using "why" as the beginning for your probe because it can be perceived as intrusive or aggressive. Instead of "Why did you select that?" try the less direct, "What were the factors and thinking that went into your selection?" Use open probes to gather information concerning facts and feelings. Some customers are sensitive to the degree of their authority. Instead of, "Are you the decision maker?" try, "Who else do you usually consult before making your decision?"

Often good probes raise more questions than they answer. Use *Follow-Up Probes* to get all the information you need, including information that is hidden, contradictory, confusing, alluded to, secret or sensitive. This is the vital information that your customer may not be comfortable sharing with you, but which may be critical to a full understanding of their needs. Examples of follow up probes are: "Say more about X. What did you mean by Y? What are the consequences of Y? How did you get involved in XX? What kind of challenges are you facing? What's the most important priority to you with this? What's the reason for that? What other issues are important to you? What would you like to see improved? How do you measure that?"

Probe wide and probe deep to get the full picture. Ask "Why..?" five times to uncover the real reason for a customer's statement. Ultimately, the goal of applying the Five Whys method is to determine a root cause of a problem. The following example demonstrates the basic process:

You: "Why the expanded operations specs? They exceed your current requirements."

Customer: "We just want to be sure we have adequate capacity."

You:	"Why?"

Customer:	"Well we might want to expand operations at some point."

You:	"Why?"

Customer:	"The market is changing and we expect to find ourselves in a growth situation."

You:	"Why?"

Customer:	(Pause). "Well, you never know, we might acquire our major competitor."

You:	"Why?"

Customer:	"They are weak in operations, which is our strength. They are strong in marketing, which is not our strength. If we acquire them, there's going to be a lot more opportunities for you guys."

Gathering Information

In the process of qualifying your candidate and in subsequent sales interviews you will begin to gather information you need to put together a presentation and/or a proposal. Probe wide and probe deep. Below are some examples.

- What prompted you/your company to look into this?

- What are your expectations/requirements for this product/ service?

- What process did you go through to determine your needs?

- How do you see this happening?

- What is it that you'd like to see accomplished?

- With whom have you had success in the past?

- With whom have you had difficulties in the past?

- Can you help me understand that a little better?

- What does that mean?

- How does that process work now?

- What challenges does that process create?

- What challenges has that created in the past?

- How did you resolve them in the past?

- What are the best things about that process?

- What other items should we discuss?

Prepare for information gathering by organizing your planned probes into categories. Figure 6, below, shows sample categories and probes. This helps ensure you get all the information you need and signals to your customer that you are organized and professional. Explain the benefit to your customer of providing you with information and access to other sources within your customer organization. Try, "Ms. Customer, the better understanding I have of your project, the better solution I will be able to propose. I would like to ask you some questions to help my understanding."

Mission and Goals	Quality	Service
What is your customer's mission, vision and values? Customer's growth strategy for the next 12 months? How do our products/ services support their strategy?	What quality standards do they expect? Have they registered complaints with us?	What service standards do they expect?
Competition	History	Decision Making
Are we a sole source? What percent? What is the market price for products/ services like ours?	Order history, volumes, products, prices Customer satisfaction Our relationship with key people	What is the decision making process? Who are the stakeholders in decisions? Who else influences decisions? Who are your advocates? Are there any against you or the project?
Culture	Legal Issues	Industry Trends
Do we understand what is "normal" negotiating? Understand what is and is not socially acceptable for the culture?	Liability Non complete, exclusivity agreements Rights to use of brands Taxes and duties	What are the current trends in the customers industry?

Figure 6: Organize your information gathering. *You will get all the information you need to create a winning proposal by following this systematic and thorough approach to your sales interviews*

To ensure full cooperation from your customer organization and to impress on decision-makers and decision-influencers your professionalism, be sure that while information gathering, take the time to build some rapport and point out how their answers will benefit their company. Briefly describe the problem you and your sponsor are partnering to solve, that you have some prepared questions you would like to ask, you would like to take notes and that it will take about xx minutes for the interview. Ask your questions systematically so that your customer understands where you are headed, thus facilitating cooperation. At the end of each category of questions, ensure that you have all the information that is there to get by asking your customer, "Is there anything else you think I should know?"

This useful open probe will sometimes bring to light some valuable information that you had not thought to ask for. At the end of the interview, ask the customer if they have any questions for you, thank them for the information, leave your business card in case they think of something later and exit promptly.

Avoid these Probes

Some types of probes you should avoid because they are ineffective or inefficient. *Doubles* are two probes joined by an "and" or a pause, which could confuse your customer. For example, "How's that report working out for you and did you see the table on page seven?" *Multiple Choice* is a set of closed-ended probes, which may not cover all the possible cases. For example, "Did you not like our service or was it the price or did you find someone else?" A *Convoluted* probe is straightforward with an unnecessary preamble. For example, "Now I know you guys have an awful lot on your plate at the moment and you are not alone by the way. All my customers are feeling the pressure, and you have probably told me this before so forgive me for asking again, but what is the deadline for proposals?" *Judgmental* probes may appear to place you in a position of superiority over your customer and can be offensive. "Doesn't that seem like a waste of time?", sounds arrogant and tactless to a customer who has spent several minutes proudly telling you about his plans. *Jargon* is terminology, much like slang, that relates to a specific activity, profession or group. It often comes across as pedantic, nerdy, and divorced from meaning to outsiders. It's best to avoid it unless you have heard your customer use it correctly herself. *Leading* probes are intended to gather objective information but have a definite bias to them. For example, "Would you describe your current process as inefficient?"

Building Rapport with Customers

Building rapport means establishing a connection between you and your candidate so that they can feel that you are like them in some way and can trust you. Connect psychologically in a simple way by shaking your customer's hand at every opportunity you get, reminding your customer that you are an authentic person and not just a role. Smiling, making eye contact and using your customer's name enhance the effect. The connection can be a shared experience in the moment or in the past, a feeling, opinion or set of values. (Avoid sharing political opinions, religious beliefs or intimate details about your life unless your customer clearly signals an invitation to do so). Sharing a laugh is especially effective. Establish the connection by finding areas of mutual interest. You can usually find something if you scan your customers office for pictures, mementos, trophies or art.

Relating stories about your everyday experiences links the intellect and the emotion. Stories about yourself, especially if they are self-deprecating, build trust by allowing your customer to get to know you as a person with strengths and vulnerabilities, like them. When your customer does the sharing, relate but don't compare. For example, when a customer tells you about the 20-inch fish he caught on the weekend, empathize with the thrill, but don't tell him about the 22-inch fish you caught. Always be polite and respectful and have a positive attitude; everybody loves a winner. Show customer data and then illustrate the data by relating a story about a customer and how they used the data, or use the Ronald Reagan technique of illustrating a data point by describing a person.

Gentle teasing is effective in disarming a customer and revealing more of your personality.

Example

Customer:	"Here's my business card."
You:	(Glancing at the job title) "How long have you been in this position, Mr. Customer?"
Customer:	"Let's see…about 18 months I guess."
You:	(Grinning) "Got the hang of it yet?" (Customer laughs)

Example:

You:	(Glancing at a sailing picture on the customer's office wall) "Are you a sailor, Mr. Customer?"
Customer:	(Big smile, turning towards the picture) "Every chance I get! I race competitively most Sunday mornings in the summer. If you haven't tried it you should; it's a rush."
You:	"Well, as a matter of fact, just this past weekend I went out on Lake Luxor with a

	couple of friends. We had a lot of laughs. The other two are experienced sailors and it seems to me that they are always out there."
Customer:	"I'd be out there a lot more often too, if this job permitted it, believe me!"
You:	"You know what Mr. Customer? I may be able to help you do just that. One of the key benefits of our service is that it saves significant amounts of time for executives - like you. (Smiling) Time you could spend sailing for instance."

Building rapport means establishing a connection between you and your customer so that they can feel that you are like them in some way. Here are some tips.

- Introduce self (company and team)

- Use customer's name early and often

- Shake hands at every opportunity

- Use simple, persuasive words

- Make eye contact, smile

- Look for areas of mutual interest

- Show genuine interest in the other person

- Share the authentic you

- Break the ice with laughter

- Be polite, respectful

- Maintain a positive attitude - everybody loves a winner

- Avoid discussing politics, religion, sex, drugs until you have built a very strong relationship

Earning your Customers Trust

If your customers perceive you as like them in some way, no matter how insignificant it may seem, they are more likely to trust you. Use rapport building to demonstrate to your customer that you have a connection with them. If they trust you, they are more likely to share qualifying information with you. One simple way to begin building trust is to share with your candidate your agenda for the meeting. It is easier to trust someone who is open about their agenda than one who hides it or is less than forthcoming. When your agenda is stated in terms of a benefit to your candidate, it has the added effect of motivating your candidate to want to cooperate. Confirm that your customer's agenda or expectations are aligned with yours before proceeding to the next step.

Understanding your customer's buying style (see the next chapter) and adjusting to it helps build a trusting relationship with your customer. When customers trust you, they readily surrender to you the critical information you need to win their business. When they trust you, they share with you their pain. And when you understand their pain, you can create a solution to ease it. Customers don't just want a solution to their problem - they want to feel good about it. They want to sleep well at night, to believe that surprises will be resolved satisfactorily, and that you have their interests at heart. Your trustworthiness is immensely valuable to your customers and they will pay for that value. If only they can find it. Customers hate buying from the lowest-cost provider. They'd far rather buy from someone they trust.

Making the Conscious Decision to Pursue

To close the qualifying part of the sales interview, first tie up any loose ends. For example, confirm names and phone numbers of other people in the account who need to be qualified. Then review any action steps that were agreed to or suggested during the call. Giving qualified candidates an assignment is an effective way to keep them invested and involved in the sales process.

Make the decision to pursue a qualified candidate a conscious one. Beware of falling into the trap of going to the next step without evaluating the opportunity. You will have qualified candidates that are qualified but may not be worth pursuing. The decision to pursue or not pursue is aimed at eliminating opportunities that you have a low probability of winning. It frees you to focus on opportunities that can be won. Your normal objective is to win the order without submitting a competitive proposal. Unfortunately, many customers must request competitive proposals by law or organizational policy. Use the pursuit decision to verify that the lead fits your organization's strategic direction and capability and that you are positioned to win. If you are responding to a RFP, check that you have addressed any unacceptable terms and conditions, unreasonable schedules and unacceptable performance warranties or penalties. Make sure that no competitor has been pre-selected and that you are not just "column fodder". Be particularly aware that the pressure of challenging quotas can lead to poor pursuit decisions and that having the resources to write proposals does not mean that you should pursue every invitation to bid. Shipley Associates, the leaders in the proposal development industry, found that improving bid discipline can double or triple your win rate, and that improving the quality of your proposals can improve your win rate by 15 to 20 percent.

A "no-pursuit" decision does not mean a lost qualified candidate. Position your qualified candidates for future opportunities by explaining to them that company resources are already committed to other projects and that you look forward to future opportunities to compete for their business.

CHAPTER 6:
READING CUSTOMER BUYING STYLES

Customers buy from people they perceive to be like them in some way

The way your customers prefer to manage their relationship with you is determined to some extent by their buying style. Your customer's *buying style* is his or her habitual, non-verbal communication with you, determined by his or her personality and buying experiences. In a similar way, your *selling style* influences the way you prefer to manage your sales relationships. Your *selling style* is your habitual, non-verbal communication with customers, determined by your personality and your sales experiences. You can improve your communication with your customers, avoid misunderstandings and conflicts, and build trusting relationships by simply understanding your customers' buying style and adjusting your approach to it.

Analyzing your Customer's Buying Style

Understand your customer's buying style by first determining if they tend to be more comfortable being outgoing or reserved. Outgoing customers tend to talk more than they listen, make statements more than they ask questions, use frequent gestures, are proactive, usually have a moderate to high energy level and tend to "think out aloud". Reserved customers are the opposite. They tend to be quiet, passive, observant, still and inscrutable. They ask thoughtful questions and do not usually share much about themselves or their ideas unless urged to do so. Your customer probably falls somewhere in between these two types because, in fact, they are on a continuum. Try and locate them predominantly at one end or the other. Your customer will generally behave according to the demands of the particular situation, making your determination about their style tendencies more challenging. For example, reserved and outgoing customers may lead a meeting in a similar, professional manner requiring that you look for subtleties to determine their style.

Next, determine if your customer prefers the company of people or tasks. People-oriented customers tend to seek others out and enjoy their company, are sensitive to the feelings of others, get much of their information about the world and draw their inspiration and energy from other people. Task-oriented customers see the world as data, processes and things, drawing their energy and inspiration from performing tasks and problem-solving. They tend to view people as sources of data or "things" to work with. This does not mean that they are not capable of being sensitive to people, because they are usually observant and interested in what makes people tick, though from a scientific/engineering viewpoint. Based on your observations of your customer, your determination should now fall within one of the following categories illustrated in Figure 7 - the Analyzer, Driver, Supporter or Influencer.

Task Oriented

Reserved   **Outgoing**

People Oriented

Figure 7: Customer buying styles and sales rep selling styles. (Adapted from Tracom Group). *Close more deals by adjusting your approach to your customer's buying style.*

Identifying the Analyzer Buying Style (Task oriented and Reserved)

Analyzers' buying decisions are logical and systematic, focused on data and facts, and conducted in a deliberate and objective manner. They respect sales reps who are knowledgeable and professional and who complete all paperwork thoroughly and accurately. They dislike being forced to make buying decisions, without adequate time, information and resources. They respond to and expect diplomacy, consideration, and respect for others. They resist having solutions forced on them - they want the data so that they can figure things out themselves. Emotionally uncontrolled situations make them very uncomfortable.

During sales interviews, Analyzers typically ask technical and thought-provoking questions about quality control.

The Analyzer's office is work-oriented, showing much activity and displays of achievement awards on the wall. They dress conservatively and make steady eye contact from an expressionless face. They choose their words carefully, speaking in a soft voice and pausing before speaking. Analyzers' movements are controlled and formal, with minimal use of gestures.

Analyzers Favorite Sayings

- nothing but the best
- there's nothing new under the sun
- proof of concept
- quality is - job#1
- an air-tight case
- are there any other options?
- it's not who you know, it's what you know
- drill down
- no pain, no gain
- analysis paralysis
- make the case for
- solid as a rock
- substantive and sustainable change
- research-proven and field-test

Selling to the Analyzer Style

Approach

- Be logical, organized and patient

- Slow it down

- Get right down to business

- Be deliberate, methodical

- Show proof for each claim

- Support your customer's principles

- Talk about documented facts

Analyzers prefer sales interviews that allow adequate time for in-depth discussion and analysis, contain proposals that are concrete, factual and well-documented and are conducted in a low-key, private but not too personal environment.

Identifying the Supporter Buying Style (People oriented and Reserved)

The Supporter's decision-making tends to be personal in nature, focused on teamwork at a measured pace. They respect people who show loyalty and appreciation, and demonstrate sincerity and concern. They dislike change, uncertainty, disorganization, interpersonal conflict and sales interviews with large groups. They typically ask about people, processes and profit, and why you believe your company is their best choice.

The Supporter's work space is warm, comfortable and inviting, displaying pictures of family and personal mementos. They tend to wear comfortable, casual and conservative clothing. Supporters will greet you with natural, warm eye contact, a pleasant and attentive smile and a warm, clasping handshake. Supporters speak slowly and calmly in soothing voices and move about gracefully.

Supporter's Favorite Sayings

- empowering

- form follows function

- what goes around comes around

- a journey of a thousand miles begins with one step

- involve all our stakeholders

- heartfelt

- there's no "I" in team

- none of us is as smart as all of us

- ready, aim, fire

- measure twice, cut once

Selling to the Supporter Style
(People oriented and Reserved)

Approach

- Be supportive

- Slow it down

- Get to know them, talk about personal life; be sociable

- Project warmth and sincerity

- Seek common areas of interest or backgrounds

- Communicate informally and casually

- Your solution should minimize the level of risk - Typically they are not risk takers.

Supporters prefer sales interviews that take into account the involvement of others, follow a standard process and propose conservative, proven solutions to problems.

Identifying the Driver Buying Style (Task oriented and Assertive)

The Driver's decision-making tends to be forceful and competitive, quick-paced, decisive and results oriented. They respect sales people who give direct answers and meet the sales challenges. They dislike poor work standards, inefficiency and slowness and routine sales procedures. They typically ask procedural and outcome oriented questions.

The Driver's workspace is organized, neat and sparsely furnished with achievement awards on the wall.

A calendar is often prominently displayed. The Driver's desk is located between the Director's and visitor's chairs. Drivers have a business-like, conservative appearance and make Intense, steady eye contact, with limited facial expressions. Their sentences are short and the structure is clipped. They tend to speak rapidly and loudly, issuing concise directives and statements. Their gestures are controlled, punchy and deliberate with an efficiency of movement. They are fond of jabbing motions with their index finger.

The Driver's Favorite Sayings

- get results

- top priority

- deal with it

- just do it
- seal the deal
- reach our goal
- quick and dirty
- turnkey operation
- if it ain't broke don't fix it
- where the rubber meets the road
- cut to the chase
- save time
- quick wins
- a slam dunk
- a tight ship

Selling to the Driver Style

In general

- Speed it up, get to the point
- Be decisive
- Be businesslike, time conscious and factual
- Show them how to reach their goal
- Project conviction and efficiency
- Talk about immediate action
- Allow them the control they need by offering a limited number of options

Drivers prefer sales interviews that are brief, to the point with a clear and obtainable objective and a one page summary of your proposal with two or three recommendations. They want very little rapport building. Notice how the sales rep matches her customer's Driver style in the following dialogue.

You: "Sounds like a wonderful opportunity, but also a lot of pressure. How will you measure success?"

Customer: "Two ways. We've got to be able to show cost savings of x million dollars and we have to hit every milestone on our launch and delivery timetable."

You: "And what do you anticipate will be the biggest obstacle to success?"

Customer: "I'd say getting every one on the same page. The people on my team are all senior executives with their own high priority projects. I don't know where some of them are going to find the time for my project."

You: "I'm beginning to see the picture. Sounds like you really have your hands full. The more I hear, the more confident I am that we can offer you and your team a system and tools that will save time in coordinating the implementation. And, project and track cost savings. Interested?"

Customer: "Maybe. Show me how it works."

You: "OK. Sure... One more, quick question. Is there funding available for this project?"

Customer: "This is the CEO's number one priority. There's plenty of money but it has not yet been allocated to specific initiatives. You make a compelling case and I'll get the money."

Identifying the Influencer Buying Style

The Influencers' decision-making style is personal and enthusiastic, quick paced, persuasive and tied to a big picture. Influencers respect sales people who collaborate with them and maintain an open mind. They typically ask who will be involved in the sales process but dislike being bogged down in details and prefer to leave the follow through to others.

The Influencer's work space is colorful and dramatic, scattered with unusual artifacts. There may be motivational pictures on the wall, the desk cluttered and messy and furniture arranged for open contact with people. They make intense, friendly but intermittent eye-contact with animated facial expressions and considerable variation in speech tone, speed and pitch. Their language tends to be rich and colorful, illustrated with frequent and expansive gestures.

The Infuencer's Favorite Sayings

- they'll love it

- make boat loads of money

- do a gut check

- feels right

- keep our options open

- a world of opportunities

- it will be fun

- blue sky it

- if it ain't broke, break it

- the biggest, the best, the most

- try something new

- the 60,000 feet view

- I feel your pain

- we'll cross that bridge when we come to it

- it's not what you know it's who you know

Selling to the Influencer Style

Approach

- Explain who is involved in the sales process

- Proceed with enthusiasm and adjustability

- Support their intentions

- Talk about people and opinions

- Be entertaining and develop a personal relationship

- Avoid too much detail, but share useful ideas that can be put into action

- Maintain a warm and sociable atmosphere

Influencers prefer sales interviews that describe the context or the big picture for your proposal. They look for creative ideas and innovative practices, and proposals that clearly connect to their personal agendas as well as the company's.

Adjusting your Approach to your Customer's Buying Style

Adjusting to customer buying styles is a selling technique which calls for you to anticipate and empathize with your customer's buying style in order to influence them. You should embed it in all of your sales practices. Adjusting applies to all stages of the sales process: converting candidates to qualified candidates, qualified candidates to customers, customers to friends, and friends to advocates.

Adjust your message to the business viewpoints of buyers, end-users, technical experts and senior managers. You must be able to see the business world through the eyes of each of these functions, and respond with the appropriate information and sales techniques. But that's not all. You must also be able to adjust to the personality, buying preferences, cultural nuances and psychological needs of each of the individuals playing the functional roles. By making this connection with the customer, you enhance your chances of winning the business.

Adjusting to the customer's way of buying reduces the likelihood of misunderstandings that often derail a sales effort. Buyers may reject your sales approach if they perceive you as too forceful, or not forceful enough; if you get bogged down in details, or if you don't pay enough attention to detail; if you are too passionate, or if you are not passionate enough; if you are too rigid, or if you are too loose. Understand their buying styles and adjust to them. Pay attention to the cues. Monitor your responses to your customer and adjust them accordingly.

To determine how to approach each style, study the tips under each style in the text above. Use the body language cues in particular, to further help identify your customer's buying style. You will probably find that you feel more comfortable with customer styles adjacent to yours. If you are a driver, for example, you'll feel more comfortable with the adjacent Analyzer style's data orientation and with the adjacent Influencer style's outgoing nature. If you are an Analyzer you'll feel comfortable with the Driver and the Supporter and so on for the other styles. Note that you are more likely to feel challenged selling to the styles diagonally opposite to yours. If you are a free-wheeling, big-thinking Influencer you may get frustrated with an Analyzer style customer's insistence on specifics and proof that your ideas will work. On the other hand, if you're a calm, thoughtful Analyzer, you may become overwhelmed by your Influencer customer's spontaneity and innovativeness. If you are a high-energy, action and goal oriented Driver, process and people oriented Supporter customers may frustrate you with their concern for inclusion and process. If you are a sensitive, caring Supporter, you'll no doubt be sensitive to the fact that you are a minority in sales and may be appalled at your Driver customer's apparent disregard for the feelings of people. Remember, that while your opposites may challenge and even fascinate you (opposites do, after all, attract), they offer you the best opportunities to improve your customer empathy and influence your customer.

Adjusting Techniques

Whether you are aware of it or not, whether you intend to or not, your body language is giving off signals that are impacting your relationship with your customers. So, the more aware you are of your body language, and the more authentic it is, the more effective your persuasive statements will be. A large part of adjusting your approach means understanding and empathizing with the feelings behind your customer's body language. Pace your customer's vocal style by listening to their speed, tone, volume and sentence length. Then without mimicking them, respond with a similar speed of voice, tone, volume and sentence length.

Without empathy, you are just miming your customer and the moment you become a mime, you lose your authenticity. Pace authentically by empathizing with your customer and allowing your natural body language to communicate your empathy. Authentic pacing will build rapport and establish a level of comfort for your customer.

Mirror your customer's basic gestures, expressions and body lean. Position yourself similarly in terms of body lean (forward, upright, and backward) and look (casual or formal). Mirror your customer's pattern of hand gesturing but not every movement. Mirror the facial signals of smiling, attending or frowning based on the content of the message. Listen and observe carefully to mirror the right facial expressions.

Signal your respect and interest by nodding, agreeing, maintaining friendly eye contact, providing three to five feet of space, squaring your body with your customer, maintaining an open posture and leaning toward your customer when appropriate. A ten percent forward lean when standing and a twenty percent forward lean when sitting creates greater rapport. Follow your customer's message with agreement cues (nodding and listening sounds) within a second or two, or your rapport will be broken.

Influencing through Body Language

Adjusting to your customer's buying style is important when it comes time to attempt to influence your customer. Remember that you must first earn the right to influence your customer through empathy. When your customer's body language indicates that they are feeling empathized with, and their verbal messages confirm it, lead them to the close by gradually shifting from body language that communicates understanding, to body language that communicates urgency.

While verbally persuading your customer, monitor the small, incremental movements your body will naturally make, pausing to see if your customer is following. If your customer begins to mirror and match your movement you can proceed towards the body language of closing, described in the chapter on Closing. This subtle technique will work only if you have successfully established synchronicity with your customer through empathy, pacing and mirroring. Otherwise, your customer will perceive your body language as manipulative and inauthentic.

Some customers are much harder than others to read. Don't get discouraged. As you spend more time with your customers, you will begin to see patterns of behavior which will clarify their buying style. If your customer's body language seems inauthentic, if it contradicts their verbal message, or if it is confusing to you, stop and ask your customer a clarifying question. Chances are that you have intercepted a mixed message from your customer. If you can successfully master the art of reading your customer's buying style and adjusting to it, you will have a competitive edge in any sales situations.

CHAPTER 7:
PREPARING AND PRESENTING
PROPOSALS TO CUSTOMERS

Nothing great was ever achieved without enthusiasm.
                    — *Ralph Waldo Emerson*

After gathering information concerning your customers' business and psychological needs, qualified them and made a decision to pursue the business, and have begun to build a trusting relationship with your customer, it's time to develop a specific proposal and presentation to win the business. To start this process, begin with the end in mind. Develop a value proposition for your customer and tie the features of your solution to specific benefits. A *Value Proposition* shows the perceived worth (value) of your products and provides your customer with reasons to buy. The key is your ability to show what the value is, how it will benefit your customer, and why it is important.

Developing a Value Proposition

Good value propositions promise to quantify anticipated improvements, specify timing of benefits, specify timing of costs, estimate the payback period—the return on investment, and specify how results will be measured and tracked. For example,

Develop value propositions collaboratively with customers. Value propositions developed with little or no customer input are more likely to be rejected. Without a thorough knowledge of your customers' needs, you can only present a generic solution, not a specific value proposition.

Next, create differentiation *statements* which compare features and benefits of your solution against those of the competition. The key to differentiation is to know what your customer wants and needs from your solution. State what differentiates your product from the competition. Show how it is a benefit, and why it is of value to your customer. For example,

You: "Our system is more versatile than our competitor's. It will allow you to make modifications on your own, without additional cost, while meeting all your requirements, including X. (Differentiator) Overall, our system will provide what you are looking for, at a lower initial cost and greater long-term value."

Here's another example:

You: "According to the National Association of XYZ Providers, the average service response time is three hours. Ours is two. (Differentiator) Our service quality standards have become the new benchmark in our industry. Last year we won the prestigious Service Excellence Award, and our methodology was recently featured in a case study in the Harvard Business Review."

Your value proposition tells your customers that your solution will solve their problem, while your differentiation statements suggest to your customer why your solution is better than your competitors. Your proposal should obviously emphasize your strengths, but you should address your weaknesses, too, before your competitors do. For example, perhaps you have developed an unfortunate reputation for missing deadlines on customer projects. You might mitigate this weakness by citing the lessons learned from a recent customer project.

Consider the example of Sodexo, a management services company, whose sales literature makes the following statements.

"Make every day a better day" (Overall Value Proposition).

"Enhancing the resident experience through resident-centered program management" (Industry-specific value proposition).

"Customer service training designed to change service behaviors and focus on resident needs" (Differentiator).

These are necessarily broad, but they guide the formulation of a "custom" value proposition for a specific customer and provide a bucket for examples of differentiators.

Never mention competitors by name. Instead, downplay their strengths and highlight their weaknesses through *ghosting*. Ghosting is simply offering a trade-off when one of the alternatives you rejected is one of the alternatives being offered by the competition. One advantage of ghosting is that you do not have to fully justify your position. You only need to create doubt. For example, you are selling training against a competitor who specializes in elearning,

You: "We were attracted to the cost-effectiveness of elearning for delivering the training but rejected it as a total solution because it does not allow for the interaction among the participants that the classroom provides. Instead we propose to blend some elearning and the classroom to deliver the training."

Or you are competing against a software reseller who has a reputation for being first in the market with new products.

You: "We considered recommending the newly-released international version of the program, which is more powerful than the standard version, but rejected it as being less user-friendly than the standard version and more challenging to maintain."

Trade-offs also show your customer that you have considered alternatives and have selected the best solution for the qualified candidate. Instead of just selecting the first available solution or your usual approach, you considered the qualified candidate's needs, risks, and budget, and offered the solution that maximizes benefits for them and minimizes their risks.

Selling with Data

Make more sales and develop ongoing authentic sales relationships through using hard data to picture market opportunities for your customers and to communicate that you understand their challenges and opportunities. First, carefully gather information that causes pain to your customers in early sales interviews. Then using industry and buying data, research opportunities to expand and/or target your customer's appeal to help your customer turn qualified candidates into customers, to get their present customers to buy more or different products and services, to get your customer to take advantage of projected trends, to modify buyer perceptions of your customer's business, to get customers to buy more or different products and services or to help your customer get their customers to buy from their web site.

Regardless of your product or service offering, there are a number of ways to show your customers how doing business with you will enable them to take advantage of the market opportunities you have identified. Spotting opportunities requires you to know your customer's business. You must be aware of all the products and services they offer to all their market segments and then show them how they can take advantage of their opportunities through strategic use of your products and services.

For example, if you are selling pictures to furniture stores, find out which furniture products are not selling and show how your pictures can draw attention to the furniture and enhance their presentation. If you are selling advertising in your magazine to restaurants, find a market segment they are missing or that is under-performing and then show them that those customers are your best readers. If you are selling business intelligence to consulting firms, show them a growing market and ask them if they are getting their share. If not, show them that the growth segment is undersupplied with business intelligence and that your products are exactly the information they are looking for. The process is always the same - picture a market opportunity, show the need for your kinds of products, why your products are best and then give them a specific proposal.

Creating Proposal Themes

Your proposal should have a *theme* that in one sentence delivers the promise of your proposal. Themes are shorter, punchier and simpler than value propositions. Consider a reseller of an automated Learning Management System that manages employee education and training. They might have the theme,

"Fewer reporting errors and smarter employees with the Socrates Learning System™".

The theme ties together the value proposition and differentiator. In the above reseller example, the value proposition is,

"Investing in the Socrates Learning System™ allows you to reduce reporting errors by at least 15% within three months and enhance employee satisfaction as measured by your annual climate survey. All without increasing current costs."

Their competitive differentiator might be,

"Our unique, customizable reports increase user satisfaction".

Link a benefit to the features of your solution, stating the benefit first, since customers are usually more interested in the benefits of your solution than its features. Add credibility to benefits by quantifying them wherever possible and supporting them with data from tests or customer experience. "Our online learning will reduce your cost" is weak compared to "You will reduce your training time from four hours to one hour through the just-in-time learning modules embedded in our learner assessment system."

Every opportunity worth pursuing warrants preparing a value proposition and a theme for your proposal. Take the time to get them right. The default strategy for every competitive situation is low price. Use it only if you are confident that your price is in fact the lowest.

Customers Buy Benefits

Customers buy benefits, not features, so you must connect the dots for them. A *feature* answers the question, "What is it?" and "How does it work?" A *benefit* answers the question, "What can it do for me?" and "So what?" A feature is only a benefit to your customer if it answers a specific, expressed need. Until then, it's simply an *advantage.* Convert features to benefits with the phrase "…which means that..." For example, "Our response time is one hour (feature), *which means that* disruption to your work-flow is kept to a minimum (advantage) improving the productivity of your claims processors (benefit)." Another example, "Our knowledge database is searchable remotely (feature), *which means that* your people can get answers to technical questions, anywhere, anytime (advantage) which will reduce those worrisome customer complaints.(benefit)".

Benefits are particularly important when responding to your customer's psychological needs. A customer may signal a psychological need by saying, "I wish, I like, I want" or "I have to, I've got to". Customers psychological needs include; opportunities for personal growth and advancement, respect, recognition, inclusion, control, and job security. While you can address psychological needs in a written proposal, your best opportunity occurs when you present your proposal. In this more personal environment you can discretely appeal to your customers' psychological and personal interests and show how your solution meets their psychological needs. This psychological appeal is vital in every decision to buy.

Remember that selling is a rational process that must be emotionalized. This means that you must, "Sell the sizzle, not the steak". Buying is an emotional process that must be rationalized, which means you must also supply proof for your claims. The following are examples of responding to key psychological needs of your customer.

You: "Our solution involves marketing, a subject you expressed interested in. (Need for growth opportunities)

You: "A recent project we completed for a large company like yours was such a success that our customer was promoted." (Need for advancement)

You: "Certainly, _Dr"._ Gonzalez . . ." (Need for respect)

You: "Our solution will raise the profile of your group within your company." (Need for recognition)

You: "You can customize the reports and get exactly the information you need when you need it. (Need for control)

You: "Stakeholder satisfaction will improve as emphasis shifts from recovery from problems to proactive organization improvement under our core service enhancements." (Need for job security)

Aligning with your customer's needs creates a bond between you and your customer. Your respectful and subtle acknowledgement of their psychological needs communicates to them that you understand their feelings. You are just like them and so they can trust you.

Respond to your customer's business needs with _functional benefits_. Functional benefits provide tangible results to your customer and fall under the broad headings of make money, save money or save time. Functional benefits address your customer's business needs, discussed in Chapter 2, What Customers Want.

Developing Standard Presentations

For consultive selling you should have a standard capabilities and a standard proposal Power Point presentation. Use the *capabilities presentation* to introduce your company and your value proposition to your customers and use the *proposal presentation* to sell them a specific, tailored solution. They should complement each other in content and style but their objectives should differ.

Use the standard capabilities presentation to get your customer's agreement that you are a legitimate player. Use it to differentiate your offerings from your competitors' and to show your overall value proposition. It should provide solid proof of your claims and eye-catching graphics that tell a story. Your capabilities presentation should be an abbreviated version of your company brochure. It should describe who you are, what you do, whom you do it for, what results you get for them and what they say about you.

Closing the deal should be the sole objective of your standard proposal. The first section should include a pick list of significant customer business needs for which you have solutions. Follow that with a value proposition formula where you plug in key benefits and measurable results including the ROI you have calculated for your customer. The main section allows you to take your customer's business needs, in order of priority to your customer, and provides solutions, expressed as benefits to the customer. It also provides proof in the form of research, testimonials, white papers, case studies or industry awards. The final section should circle back to your value proposition and ask for the order. Like your capabilities presentation, your standard Power Point proposal should be an abbreviated version of your standard written proposal. A standard proposal planner like the one in Figure 8 helps you build a winning proposal while saving you time reinventing the wheel.

Standard Proposal Planner
1. Customer's Challenge or Opportunity and Your Value Proposition
2. Customer Business and Psychological Needs, (priority ranked)
3. Your Solution to Customer Needs Need #1 • Your Solution • Benefits & Features • Proof • Supporting Graphics Need # 2 • Your Solution • Benefits & Features • Proof • Supporting Graphics Need # 3 • Your Solution • Benefits & Features • Proof • Supporting Graphics
4. Summary • Restate value proposition • Close on Next Steps
Sample of a Completed Proposal Planner
1. Customer's Challenge or Opportunity and Your Value Proposition The City of Candoville can enhance its ability to deliver employees' Individual Development Plans (IDP)s and accelerate employee development and succession planning in support of its "One City" vision by choosing Organization Development Solutions (ODS) to design an employee development planning course for City leaders, managers and supervisors.
2. Customer Business and Psychological Needs, priority ranked • Individual direct reports acquire knowledge, attitudes and skills that reflect real, prioritized organizational needs. • City managers must identify organizational competency gaps for use in management development and succession planning. • Competitive pricing.

3. **Your Solution to Customer Needs**
    Need #1
    The City's employee development planning must ensure that individual direct reports acquire knowledge, attitudes and skills that reflect real, prioritized organizational needs.

    Your Solution
    ODS will design an online or self-paced course and process that teaches City leaders, managers and supervisors how to lead employees through a self-development process. This comprehensive, step by step approach to learning employee development planning gives leaders the confidence and the competence to guide their direct reports to produce effective development plans.

    Benefits
    - Increased likelihood that employees will complete meaningful and actionable Individual Development Plans (IDP)s.
    - Open and positive communication between managers and direct reports.
    - Increased striving for personal excellence among all City employees.
    - Greater utilization of the City's existing Professional Development Programs.

    Features
    - Integration of the City's existing Skill Set Questionnaire, a development tool that asks specific questions related to their career goals.
    - Measures of success for development plans and their implementation.
    - Employee selection of learning activities that match their learning styles.

    Proof
    This approach resulted in 95% completion rate of IDPs at ABC County and XYZ Pharmaceuticals

    Supporting Graphics
    Picture of manager coaching an employee to complete a IDP.

Need # 2

City managers must identify organizational competency gaps for use in management development and succession planning.

Your Solution

A training section on Gap Prioritization. Learning objectives include:
- How to conduct a Gap Analysis
- How to prioritize gaps before selecting development activities
- Use of simple skill vs. importance rating to identify priority of development gaps

Benefits & Features
- Enhanced capability of the City to meet current and future job succession needs
- The sectional design of the course enables City leaders to take the course in as little as an hour, thus increasing the likelihood that they will complete it. The samples, tools and job aids make it easy for them to implement the development planning with their direct reports.

Proof

This approach resulted in ABC implementing a succession plan and a management development plan shortly after completion of the gap analysis and Individual Development Plans.

Supporting Graphics
- Hand written Testimonial on ABC City letterhead.

Need # 3

Competitive pricing.

Solution

Customized and reproducible Leader's Guide ....$ 6000
Customized and reproducible Employee's Guide ....$ 3500
Total for project ....
........................$ 9500

Benefit

Our transparent pricing mitigates your risk. The price per leader for the course is almost negligible, while the financial impact of employee development planning on the City could be measured in the hundreds of thousands of dollars.

3. Summary

Restate value proposition

The City of Candoville can enhance its ability to deliver employees' Individual Development Plans (IDP)s and accelerate employee development and succession planning in support of its "One City" vision by choosing Organization Development Solutions to design an employee development planning course for City leaders, managers and supervisors.

Close on Next Steps

Get us a Purchase Order number so that the City can begin realizing the benefits.

Figure 8: Standard Proposal Planner, adapted from Shipley Associates. *Use this proven organizer to outline all your proposals, informal or formal, written or verbal, large or small*

Much of your selling process takes place virtually, through e-mail, phone, and other electronic communication. Once you have a chance to formally present, face-to-face or electronically with a customer, you had better make a good impression. You generally can't win significant business without a sales presentation, even if you need to rely on a virtual medium for presenting.

Preparing for your Presentation

Preparation of a proposal requires more time and effort than many sales organizations realize. Just because you know your company's offerings inside out and you have studied your customer's industry does not mean that you can pull together a presentation during a coffee break. You may be able to talk for hours about the benefits of your products, your marketing department may have some powerful presentations you can use and your website may be an award winner. You still must prepare. You must prepare and rehearse a presentation that will influence a specific customer or group of customers. This means customizing the content, the message and the "look and feel" for your customer and/or the venue. Having some good standard presentations as templates helps reduce the time.

Managing Your Managers

Assert your leadership role as the owner of the account with senior managers from your company, no matter how senior they might be. You should proactively schedule the meetings with the customer, and the briefing meetings with you. Never allow a senior manager to meet with anyone in the customer organization without consulting you first. You, not the manager, should decide on the meeting agenda. You should coach the managers on what to do, what to wear, what to say and, perhaps more importantly, what not to say. Tell them where you are in the project plan, and discuss with them in depth the needs and expectations of the customer they are meeting with. Role-play the meeting with them. Help them to focus on the needs of the customer. Coach them to defer questions to you that are outside their area.

Preferably, you should accompany your managers to the meeting. Introduce them to the customer (not vice-versa) and confirm the objectives and agenda for the meeting. The format of the meetings is less important. They can be one-on-one or team meetings. They can be in the board room or in a restaurant. They must, however, be well prepared and well orchestrated meetings. Make sure that you have a pre-arranged signal with your managers to indicate when they are getting off track. If you need to interrupt them, do it politely but firmly. You, not your manager nor your customer, must control the meeting. Managing relationships is fraught with pitfalls. Problems can include wishing, hoping and assuming that relationships are just fine, losing sight of the forest for the trees, losing sight of the trees for the forest or, "The Lone Ranger" syndrome; I can do it all myself.

Focusing your Presentation on your Customer

Understand the needs of your stakeholders and make sure your presentation addresses them. Align your presentation plan with your customers' strategic vision of your proposed solution. Presenting features and demonstrating capabilities alone is ineffective. You need to differentiate your message by linking your solution to real customer benefits. Be clear and logical. Your customers want to see proof that your solution works for them. Choose psychological and persuasive words like *more, success, new, increased, genius, improved, exciting, enormous, genuine, durable, effective, money* and *profit.* Choose words and phrases familiar to the customer, while keeping in mind Winston Churchill's insistence that "the familiar words are best, and when short, are best of all".

Group your points in threes or sevens. Western folklore has the 'rule of three'. Three strikes you're out. Three riddles are asked. Good things come in threes. A triangle has three points. Three reasons are easy to recall. Seven has magical and biblical connotations. God created the world in six days and on the seventh He rested. Seven points are more intriguing than eight and seven is easy to remember. (That is why USA phone numbers have seven digits.)

Complex sales require extended time and multiple contacts. Customer needs, issues and assumptions change and evolve. Validate your assumptions and understandings repeatedly. Since value is determined by the customer, you must collaborate to determine what this customer values. Use your collaborative relationship to validate your solution before finalizing your proposal. Solutions that have been validated by your customer usually win.

You: "Ms. Customer, the purpose of today's meeting is for you to evaluate how our portfolio of products and services can support your department's policy-making and executive decisions. To recap, as you suggested, we conducted an extensive survey of your key executives to determine their current sources of business information. We reviewed the results with you and identified where decision-support information appeared to be less than adequate. Based on that analysis we have prepared some pre-proposal recommendations which we will share with you today. Is this more or less what you expected to have happen today?"

In a formal sales presentation you must learn beforehand who your customer-audience will include - their names, job function and hot buttons. Know your sales presentation objectives and what action you want your customer to take after your presentation. Do you want them to sign a contract, an order form, a letter of intent or your written proposal, or is there another necessary step before the close, like a trial installation or a pilot test?

When invited to make a formal presentation, determine your room set-up needs and get them to your customer or inside sponsor well in advance. Find out if you can control the heating/cooling and lighting in the room where you will present. Bring your own laptop and data projector to mitigate the risk of technical difficulties. If possible, visit the room in advance to verify its suitability. Is it large enough for the size of the group, or, equally problematic, is it too large? Are there enough chairs, will there be water on the table and writing materials available? Are there slide screens and whiteboards with markers and an eraser? Arrange for coffee since caffeine enhances alertness and camaraderie, paving the way for you to engage and persuade them.

Your customer's retention of information, your credibility, and your effectiveness depend on effective use of visuals during your sales presentation. However, over-used graphics and visuals can become a distraction and be seen by the customer as a "crutch". Choose graphics and visuals that show customers using your products. Color can accelerate retention so use it to highlight key points. Test the colors to see how they project. Use blue for headings, black for the body content and red or green for highlighting. Use plenty of "white" space for readability, putting no more than 5 or 6 lines per slide. Focus on the few visuals that show the facts and figures that support or prove your key points. Mix it up by using bulleted lists, anagrams, tables, bar charts, line charts, pie charts, flow charts and pictures. Use flip charts or white boards for collaborative work with customers during your presentation.

Rehearse your presentation at least five times. While you do not need to memorize the entire presentation word for word, you should be able to recall without notes the sequence of topics and key points.

Delivering your Presentation

Psych yourself up for your sales interview or presentation by boosting your mental edge. Visualize yourself delivering a winning presentation. To regain your energy and alertness if you have been sitting in an airplane or car for more than an hour, drink some coffee and go for a brisk walk.

If you tend to get nervous before a formal presentation, remember that a little anxiety is a good thing because it supplies energy. However, too much nervousness can be debilitating. Stand at the door and greet people as they enter. Shake hands. Meet your customer-audience, break the ice and make some friends.

If you have an anxiety attack, focus on your breathing and hold onto something long enough to steady your hands and arms. But don't become permanently attached. Remind yourself that no-one wants you to fail; everyone wants you to deliver a good (but not perfect) presentation. Think of your presentation as a gift to your customer; it is about your customer, not your performance. Don't apologize for nervousness. Chances are your customer hasn't even noticed. Memorize your opening sentence, so that you get off to good start. Talk to the friendly faces first (there is always at least one friendly face), gradually expanding to the entire group as your confidence grows.

Introducing your Presentation

Customers are most attentive at the very beginning and the end of your presentation, so make sure you get your message across at both those points.

Introduce your presentation by defining the situation and the problem/opportunity it presents for your customer, and the benefits or consequences of solving it, while establishing some rapport with your customers. The introduction is a lot to accomplish and you have just a few minutes to do it. Spice up your opening with a relevant personal anecdote, a startling statistic, a strong quote or a brief story or parable. To enhance your credibility, emphasize collaboration with people in the customer organization. Take care to state your purpose or reason for your presentation in terms of a benefit to your customer and confirm their expectations for the meeting. Build rapport with your customers by introducing yourself and any team members with you, use each customer's name early and often, smile and make eye contact with individuals, find an area of mutual interest (even if it's just lunch or the weather) and kick off your presentation in a conversational and upbeat tone. You must be upbeat. If you are not enthusiastic about your value proposition, you cannot expect your customer to be.

Never begin with an apology. Don't say, "I am sorry that I was unable to schedule our CEO for this meeting, but___." Customers tend to disregard everything you say before the word "but" and respond to what comes after. Avoid the word "but". Even if you are there to apologize, open with something positive, then transition to the bad news. Disclose in advance, or concede negative points that are likely to come out and be sure to point out disadvantages or risks and how you will mitigate them. Disclosing in advance likely negatives enhances your credibility on other points.

Presenting the Body of your Presentation

The body is the "meat" of your presentation and also the time when your customer's attention is most likely to wander. Begin the meat of your presentation with your value proposition. Your task then is to sell your solution, while keeping your customers engaged. An effective way to accomplish both objectives is to organize the body by customer needs and or similarities (example: quality service and price). Starting with your customers' most pressing need, express each key point as a benefit to the customer but always state the benefit first and then describe the features. Remember, customers buy benefits not features so follow this up with proof of your claim. Proof may be a research report, a case study, a testimonial, an exhibit or demonstration, white papers, media coverage, or logical argument.

Beginning the Ending of your Presentation

Begin the ending by summarizing your presentation and emphasizing the benefits of your solution. You can inject life into it with a motivational quote, a story or parable about a customer who selected your solution and enjoyed its benefits or visualizing the future for your customer. If it's not appropriate to ask for the order, then get your customer's commitment to the next steps. Keep the momentum going by asking them to complete some assignment between steps, even if it's just a minor task.

At the end of a formal presentation you should expect and look forward to questions from customers. Questions are a valuable opportunity for clarifying and reinforcing your main points and strengthening trust. As you are planning your presentation, schedule time for questions and answers that will add support to your message. When you get a question, restate it (clarifying), give a bottom-line answer concisely, support your answer, summarize your main point, and ask if the questioner is satisfied. Respond to one question at a time and listen very carefully to the tone and wording of the question. Use eye contact and movement to demonstrate interest to the questioner. If you can't answer the question, admit it and move ahead with the next question.

Monitoring your Customer's Response

Customers respond to your sales presentation verbally and non-verbally (*body language*). When faced with a contradiction between someone's words and their body language, our intuition tells us to go with the message communicated non-verbally. Pay attention to your customers' body language to recognize when they are agreeing, resisting, skeptical or ready to be closed. As Yogi Berra said, "You can see a lot just by watching." If you are to pick up and respond to these subtle messages, you must keep your eyes on your customer without staring, which can be seen as a strong desire for control.

If your customer is comfortable with the direction that your sales presentation is taking, you should continue as planned. Watch for changes in your customer's energy level, body movements and language style. Change may indicate that your customer is reacting on some level to what you are saying or doing. It might be an unspoken objection or it could be a buying signal. Stop whatever you were doing or saying and ask a question. On the telephone your customers might change their voice tone, speed or volume, or there may be a long pause. A pause, even a long pause, doesn't always mean the customer has said everything. Remember you earn the right to interrupt by first listening and seeking to understand.

It is better to have your customer's communication in words than go unspoken and pop up at an inconvenient time, like at the close for example. Don't state that you noticed that your customer squirmed when you mentioned price. Simply ask them if what you are saying is making sense, or if they have a question. If there is no issue, your customer will tell you to continue. If there is an unspoken issue, you have provided your customer the opportunity to get it out on the table.

Remember too that it's normal for a customer to have mixed feelings about new ideas or proposals. Hesitations, lingering doubts, confusion or anxiety may be expressed through body language, even as your customer is giving you positive verbal messages. Customers may try to restrain their interest or enthusiasm for fear of losing a negotiating edge. Usually though, their true feelings will leak our through their body language. Your attentive reading of your customer's body language will improve your understanding of their needs, clue you into their hot buttons and be a rich source of feedback for you about their receptivity to you and your ideas.

While the real value of observing your customer's body language is to pick up on mixed messages or changes in patterns of movements plus getting your customer to verbalize the issue, you may attempt to interpret specific body language without seeking verification. The table below provides interpretation for some typical body language of western cultures during a sales interview. Interpretations may be different in other cultures.

Body Region	Customer's Body Language	Possible Meaning(in Western cultures only)
Eyes	Intent staring	"I want to control you and the agenda"
	Avoiding your eyes	"I'm uncomfortable with you" or "I'm trying to hide something from you"
	A sparkle or glint in the eye	"This is interesting!" or "I'm enjoying this relationship"
	Glassy-eyed	"I'm bored"
	Looking up and to the side	"I wonder how that might work for me?"
	Looking sideways	"Where have I heard that before?"
	Casting their eyes down	Experiencing some emotional discomfort
	Shifting eyes	Lying or looking for a way out
	Glancing towards the door	"I want this meeting to be over."
	Glancing towards an object in the room	"I want to talk about (the object)"
Hands	Drumming their fingers	Impatience - "Get to the point"
	Hands in the shape of a steeple with fingertips touching	Evaluating you, your work or your company
	Playing with a pen or pencil, shuffling papers	Concerned, annoyed, confused or wanting to say something

	Pointing at you, jabbing the desk with their finger	Angry or frustrated
	One hand tightly holding the other wrist down	On guard, threatened or very cautious
	Touching, picking up or caressing your product	Buying signal!
Face	Lightly rubbing the side of the nose with a finger when talking	Lying or at least, not sure of the veracity of what they are telling you
	Stroking the chin	Reflecting on what you are saying
Arms	Folded across the chest in a formal meeting	Protecting information or feelings
	Folded across the chest in an informal meeting	Relaxed
	One hand on the arm of the chair, the other elbow crooked and weight leaning on it	Want to get up and leave
	Hands lightly crossed or open, resting on the desk	Interested, trusting
Posture	Leaning back	Wanting to distance themselves from you
	Leaning forward	Interested
	Bolt upright, stiff	Seeking to gain control of the meeting

Figure 9: Your Customer's Body Language Means Business *Before jumping to conclusions try to verify the meaning of your customer's non-verbal communication by getting them to verbalize it*

Your wardrobe should be appropriate for the occasion so take your cue from your sponsor and dress to his/her standard or a touch above it.

Your voice is a powerful tool. Monitor and vary its speed, tone, volume and clarity. Avoid sing-song, monotones and voice trailing off at the end of sentences. Pause slightly before a word that is technical or foreign to your audience, including the names of people and places. You may need to practice projecting your voice for large rooms or large groups but beware of shouting. Use a microphone if necessary. Your voice must convey enthusiasm (the word comes from Greek, meaning "in God"), conviction, confidence, interest and concern. Impeccable manners are crucial, of course, as is sounding alert, expressive, natural, friendly and distinct. Choose your words carefully, recognizing that they are powerful tools, which can have a positive or negative impact on your customer. Your choice of words should match your customer's buying style, containing more "you" than "I".

Take a deep breath before you speak so you're able to lower your pitch and to help sound authoritative. Rid yourself of irritating speech habits, like, "um", "er", "you know", which convey only insecurity. Build rapport and trust by trying to match your rate of speech to your customers'. Customers love to hear the sound of their own name so use it early and often – but don't let it sound forced or false. Ensure that your customers hear the names of products, people or places by pausing slightly after enunciating the word.

Pay attention to your body language to maximize your impact and mitigate the risk of sending mixed messages. Practice using the following gestures to emphasize your points:

Your Intent	Use this Gesture
Show determination	Clench your fist
Caution your customer	Point Index finger outwards, but not directly at your customer
Categorize, separate ideas	Slice the air in front of you with your hand
Compare, contrast ideas	Locate the ideas in space to your left and right
Reject an idea	Fold your arms, or push it away
Emphasize a point	Step forward, point, pause
Involve your audience	Make eye contact, open body posture

Figure 10: Use Gestures in your Presentation *Make sure that your gestures reinforce and don't contradict your verbal message*

Managing Questions after your Presentation

Expect and look forward to questions from your customers. Questions are often a valuable sales opportunity for clarifying and reinforcing main points. When planning your presentation, schedule time for questions and answers. If you have an hour, limit your presentation to 40 minutes, allowing 20 minutes for questions. To organize your response to questions, give a concise answer offering proof or support, summarize your main point and ask if the questioner is satisfied. Respond to one question at a time and listen very carefully to the tone and wording of the question. Use eye contact to demonstrate interest in the question. If you can't answer the question, admit it and move ahead to the next question.

Influencing Your Customer

The difference between influencing your customers and manipulating them is in your intent. If you have their best interests at heart, then you are influencing them. If you are out to take advantage of them you are probably manipulating them. For example, you might persuade your customer to purchase a service contract because you know that their own service technicians do not have the time to do it. That would be influencing. If, on the other hand, you persuaded your customer to purchase a service contract, knowing that your customer's organization was fully capable of doing it themselves and knowing that you would get a special bonus for selling service contracts this month only, you might just be manipulating your customer. To have an authentic business relationship with your customer, to be your authentic self while selling, it's better to influence, rather than manipulate your customer.

Your power to influence your customer's decisions, opinions, assumptions and even values comes from your role or job title, your expertise, credentials or reputation, your relationship with your customer and your skills in presenting your ideas, solutions or recommendations. Customers use emotion and logic to make decisions and you must be able to influence both by providing reasons to buy and by appealing to psychological needs.

Persuade your customer by connecting all the features of your product/solution to your customer's needs. Don't rely on features alone. Clearly link your customers' business and psychological needs to your solution. Assume your customer is hearing your solution for the first time, even though they may have read about it or heard you speak about it before.

Position yourself as your customer's ally by emphasizing your independence or neutrality. Minimize your self-interest to enhance credibility. For example, "I get no commission or bonus from this, but if I were you, I would seriously consider ____." Maintain your credibility by adhering to established ethical standards, introducing appropriate company experts and senior managers, substantiating claims, and staying on point with your message.

Buying and selling is an emotional business whether or not your customers acknowledge it. You can greatly improve your influencing skills by using emotion-based appeals that prompt customers to drop their natural defenses. The same appeals require less effort than logic, and are usually more interesting and easier to recall than data, especially if you can involve all five senses. President Reagan made sweeping changes to the US welfare system by telling emotional stories about "The Welfare Queen." Oprah influences millions every week through skilled weaving of emotion and logic. In the buttoned-down corporate world, where overt expression of emotion is frowned upon, you have to be subtle about it. Quietly reminding customers of their deadlines may elicit an emotion that gets them moving forward. Including slides showing customers clearly enjoying the benefits of your solution and using emotional words such as *love, enjoy, happy, delighted, celebration, recognition, rewards* may elicit more positive emotions.

Adjust your presentation style to your customers. If it's a formal presentation, clarify your customers' expectations beforehand. In most cases, you can collaborate with your customer as you develop your presentation. Don't be afraid of repeating your message again and again. Remember that advertising works when the message is frequent and consistent.

Refrains and slogans are effective. In the famous O.J. Simpson trial, O.J.'s attorney influenced the jury with refrains like, "If the glove does not fit, you must acquit." Golfers say, "Drive for show, putt for dough." Sales trainers like, "the ABCs - Always Be Closing." Franchises are sold with, "In business for yourself, but not by yourself." President Roosevelt famously sold the USA on assisting England at the beginning of World War 2 by comparing his complicated lend/lease plan to, "Lending your hose to your neighbor when his house is on fire." Be creative by finding a slogan, metaphor or refrain that represents key messages in your proposal.

Story-telling is an ancient influencing skill which leaders have used for centuries. For example, Jesus Christ told parables (i.e. stories) to persuade his followers to adopt his values and spread his message. Aesop told fables and the Grimm brothers told fairy tales to influence the behavior of children. Tell stories about how your best customers were skeptical at first but delighted when they bought from you. Tell them how your product/service saved money/made money for a customer who was on the brink of disaster, or who was at the peak of success. Don't just give them the facts. Spin a story by making the people come alive and by dramatizing the problem your solution solved. Give your story a beginning, middle and end. Tell them what the problem was like for your customer, what happened and what it is like now as a result of your solution. Gather stories about the legends in business like Jack Welch, Henry Ford, Bill Gates, Oprah Winfrey and J.P. Morgan and apply them to your customer's needs and your solution.

Selling Against your Competition

Do not criticize your competitors or their products in front of your customer. Customers may see you as unprofessional and unfair. However, you can imply that your competitors are offering a problematic solution without naming them. *Ghosting* is a technique that calls attention to a competitor's weakness by highlighting the problems associated with their approach or product without mentioning names. For example,

> You: "Access to our award-winning Online University means that your new hires can get up to speed immediately on our systems and tools, without having to wait around for the next scheduled class."

This statement implies that the classroom is inferior to online learning. If you know that your competitor does not offer online learning, then you have given your customer a reason to reject their proposal. You could strengthen your statement by saying,

> You: "While considering the most productive way to train your new hires on our systems and tool we considered traditional classroom learning but rejected it as less cost-efficient than e-learning."

Here you have strengthened your credibility and your solution, while implying that your competitors are not thinking about your customers needs when proposing classroom style training.

Up-selling and Cross-selling

If you've been probing, listening and solving problems for your customer throughout your sales presentation, the next step, up-selling and cross-selling, should come naturally. The idea is actually to resell your customer, not only to increase sales, but also to ensure that your customer has no reason to turn to your competition. Your objective is to become your customer's sole supplier of your product line.

Don't be reluctant about this phase of the sales cycle. Your customer has already invested time with you, and has decided to buy your product or service. An up-selling/cross-selling message will not fall on unreceptive ears. If you're not regularly up-selling and cross-selling, perhaps you feel that you're already getting enough business from you customer, or you have convinced yourself that it's safer to leave well enough alone or you think that your customer knows your company well enough to request more of your product if he or she wanted it, or you assume that your customer has a reason for passing up part of your product line without having discussed it or you simply lack the courage to suggest a larger order, after selling your customer a single product. There's no doubt that, "Would you like fries with that" has worked well for McDonalds.

Other barriers to up-selling and cross-selling are identical to those that hinder the primary sales interview. We don't listen for opportunities throughout the sales presentation to up-sell or cross-sell. We sell features, instead of benefits, or oversell without meeting customer expectations. Remember, that your goal is to develop a long-term partnership with your customer. Up-selling and cross-selling are important factors in fostering and maintaining that relationship. In fact, up-selling and cross-selling should be part of your sales interview objectives. But, you'll need to be creative. Try brainstorming with your sales manager, your colleagues, your product manager or your marketing manager. Read trade publications that reflect trends in your customer's business that could have an impact on their needs. Get your sponsor to set up meetings with customer end-users who are satisfied with a wide range of your products to determine how each item is used. In short, keep probing for your customer's business problems, develop a solution and then explore ways in which other products or service lines can enhance your value proposition.

Present up-sells or cross-sells in your proposal as options that enhance your value proposition. Naturally you will first focus on closing your customer on your customer need-driven solution. When you have gained agreement on your solution, introduce the benefits of your up/cross-sell and get a further agreement with, for example, "How does that sound?" Follow up with a trail close such as, "If I gave you a price break on that item combined with your original order, would you be interested?" Presuming your customer has been receptive thus far, use an assumptive close like,

"We'll add that item to your original order and get it right out to you Wednesday morning."

You should anticipate a sales presentation early in the sales cycle, design your message with clarity and conciseness, use only effective visuals, and develop and practice an effective style.

CHAPTER 8:
MANAGING CUSTOMER OBJECTIONS

Any fear is an illusion. You think something is standing in your way, but nothing is really there. What is there is an opportunity to do your best and gain some success. If it turns out that my best isn't good enough, then at least I'll never be able to look back and say I was too afraid to try.

—*Michael Jordan*

An *objection* is a customer's resistance to your proposal. Customers object for many reasons, all of which have one thing in common - the fit between your customer's problem and your proposed solution is less than perfect. An objection should not be interpreted as rejection, or as a sign of failure, but rather as an important message from your customer. Think of objections as requests for more information. In other words, they are asking, "Tell me how to justify this expenditure?", "What return can we expect on this investment?", "Tell us how your other customers have dealt with their price concerns?" or "What guarantee can you offer that it will work?"

Identifying the Type of Objections

A useful way to manage objections is to first identify the objection's type. If it's a *request for more information,* then simply provide that information in terms of benefits to your customer. Consider the objection, "We don't need any help thanks very much. We have our own process and it works very well." Convert the objection to a question and you get, "Explain to me how your process is superior to our current one."

Or your customer may be under a *misconception* concerning your solution. For example, "I'm sorry but your system's lack of scalability rules it out." Offer the correct information with proof - "You'll be happy to know that in fact our system has infinite scalability, as this graphic shows."

Another type of objection is the *complaint,* perhaps leftover from your customer's past experience with your company or its products. For example, "We hired your company last year and there were hours of meetings and no results. They didn't understand our business." This is actually another request for more information, "Tell me how you are going to learn about our business." The key to managing this type of objection is to show empathy and then to share your new improved and streamlined methodology for getting up to speed on your customer's business issues.

A slightly tougher type of objection is *skepticism.* Your customer doubts the validity of your claims. For example, "Nice theory and clearly you have put a lot of effort into developing your system but it won't work here." In terms of a request for information, your customer is asking you to show him where your system has had success in an operation like his. He's demanding proof of your claim. You must be ready to offer a case study, a testimonial, a white paper, independent research, the endorsement of a well-known industry expert, an industry award your product has won or extensive coverage by the media.

The toughest objection of all comes from the *cynical* customer. The cynical customer does not believe your claim or your proof. For example, "This is just another fad some consultants sold you guys for a billion dollars.

Your company is such a fat target for consultants. You never learn." The cynical objection is not a request for more information. Your customer will always find fault with it. He simply does not trust you, your solution or your company. Fortunately, you can win over your cynical customer by providing the opportunity for him to hear your value proposition and its proof from someone he does trust. This might be his counterpart in another customer's organization who is satisfied with your solution and is willing to talk to your customers, or a third party expert of his choosing. Be prepared to offer him a name and a phone number, on the spot if possible.

Note how the sales person uses empathy, information, testimonials and third party references to overcome misconceptions, skepticism and cynicism in the following dialogue which picks up midway through an exploratory sales interview.

Customer: "We are working on an RFP for an Executive Information System. It's a major initiative with ramifications for our entire way of operating internally, not to mention its impact on service delivery quality. I believe that the shock waves will be felt throughout the entire state, maybe even to the federal level. (Grimacing) But I don't think you guys could handle a project of this size and scope."

You: "What makes you think that Michael?"

Customer: "Well your firm's core competence is strategic IT consulting – and you are excellent at it – but this is more nuts and bolts, you know, systems integration and maintenance, not quite your cup of tea."

You:

"You are absolutely correct, a year ago. You probably haven't heard yet about our acquisition of Slick Systems Integrators. SSI, as you may know, is a leading player in the systems integration space. The acquisition is a real coupe for us. Would you agree that the acquisition qualifies us to bid on your project?"

Customer:

"Wow. That is interesting. (Leans back, frowning, and folding his arms) I hate to be a wet blanket, but I have seen a lot of mergers and acquisitions fail to deliver on their promises, and worse, fail their customers in the process. Now don't take this personally, but I am very reluctant to allow this company to be a guinea pig in this experiment."

You:

"I don't blame you for being skeptical. Actually, other customers have felt the same. However, when they investigated the new company further, they found that the quality and reliability of service has actually improved since the acquisition." (You reach into your briefcase, take out a document on letterhead and slide it across the desk). "Look, here's a letter from a customer, complimenting us on our performance." (Customer glances at it, but does not pick it up.)

You:

"You are still not comfortable with it, are you? I can understand your reluctance. I sit in your office and tell you that we can do this project for you, I show you a letter from a customer, but those nagging doubts are still there, aren't they?" (Arms still crossed Customer shrugs apologetically.)

You: "What if I arranged for you to speak personally and privately with a customer about their experience of our services, would that help ease your mind?"

Customer: (Uncrosses his arms, smiles, then energetically leans across the desk, hand extended). "You are a persistent son of a gun. OK. I'll talk to your customer, and if he confirms all that you say, you'll have my blessing."

Reading the Body Language of Objections

When your customer is resistant, confused, or has an objection, you should stop talking and ask a question. You will recognize an unspoken objection when your customer abruptly changes posture, eye contact or facial expression, when language style changes to more formal, less conversational and when voice speed, pitch and volume seem more controlled. Your customer's eyes may break off contact with yours, and become fixed on an object in the room, look out the window, or glance towards the door. Frowning, grimacing or turning up the nose obviously indicates that they are not happy with something you have said or done. Muscles may tense up, they may fidget with a pen, or drum their fingers on the desk. They may shift position, draw a sharp breath, cough or clear the throat. Body lean may shift back and away from you. Arms may cross, or hands come up in a "stop" or "slow down" gesture.

In some instances your customer may be annoyed with you, offended or have a strong objection or complaint. He does not want you to continue, and may want to end the meeting. You should immediately stop whatever you are doing or saying and ask a question. Watch for low, listless energy level. Your customer's language style may become formal and officious with short, measured sentences. Your customer may use technical words or jargon, accompanied by generalities and euphemisms. Her voice may be pitched a little higher, with hints of defensiveness, irritation, criticism, sarcasm or cynicism. Eyes may stare stonily into yours or they avoid eye contact with you, looking down, or looking past you while talking. Muscles may be still, but coiled, ready to get up from the chair. You may notice tightening or twitching of the facial muscles, or clenching the jaw. Your customer may lean away from you or turn her shoulder towards you - "the cold shoulder".

Process for Overcoming Objections

Objections can occur anywhere along the sales process, though most often they occur after your presentation. Overcoming objections paves the way for the close. If you have removed all remaining questions from the customer's mind and you have proven the value of your proposition, you have earned the right to ask for the order. Objections are painful only if you are not prepared with information, or if you are not skilled in this practice. Similarly, closing is painful only when you have not earned the right.

Getting to the "Real" Objection

Listen to get to the truth of the objection. Don't get defensive, even if your customer is aggressive. Defensiveness signals to your customer that you may be trying to hide something, that you do not believe in your proposal or that you are less than professional. Customers sometimes miss the need-benefit connection. Have you probed and listened to your customer's needs? Have you focused on the benefits of your product that have a direct impact on your customer? Are you presenting benefits in a clear, concise fashion, in terms of meeting needs and solving problems?

Customers can lose sight of the goal. In the heat of the sales interview, a peripheral issue may sidetrack your customer. You're talking about pricing and your customer abruptly begins to grumble about past delivery problems. You find that the discussion is veering out of your control. Listen with empathy and gently guide your customer back to their objectives. Customers screen out salespeople who waste time. Perhaps your customer is indeed too busy to talk to you or is frustrated with time-wasting salespeople and has automatically assigned you to that category.

Keep in mind that your customer's feelings can interfere with their reasoning, leading them to reject risky propositions. When it perceives ambiguity or the qualified candidate of losing money, the brain releases chemicals that produce feelings of fear. When your customer appears to be uncertain, confused or emotional, show how your proposal mitigates the risk of losing money.

Sometimes your customer does not have enough reasons to buy. Does your customer say she can't afford your product, when, in fact, she's considering buying from your competition? Is your customer citing satisfaction with his present supplier just because it's easier to maintain the status quo than to confront change? Perhaps your customer perceives a very real obstacle that prevents him from committing to your product. If it's real, and you have responded to it, you can confidently close by asking for the order. As you build your customer base, you'll hear certain objections over and over again. They can help you refine your sales message and address objections routinely.

Example 1

Customer: "Not ready yet. Call me back after the budgeting cycle is over."

You: "I certainly could do that. My concern for you is that it's difficult to budget for something unless you know what you need. Let's invest some time now analyzing your needs so that you will have a better idea of what to budget later."

Example 2

Customer: "I need time to think about it."

You: "Of course. Do you mind sharing with me what specific things you need to think over? Perhaps I can set your mind at rest here and now."

Example 3

Customer: "I'm satisfied with my existing supplier."

You: "How did that relationship begin?"
"What criteria did you use to select them?"
"What do you like about them?"
"What could they improve?"
"Would you give me the same opportunity you gave your current supplier back when you gave them their first order?"

Probe for objections that you can expect your customer to raise. For example, your customer says, "Your product sounds fine, but I can't afford it. My budget's been cut." Don't respond, "Sorry to hear that. I'll check back in a few months to see if your situation has changed." Continue to probe. While your customer may indeed not be able to afford your product, there's also a chance that your product can improve productivity. Perhaps you have a deferred payment or leasing plan. Maybe your customer doesn't want your product and figures a "budget" story will get you off the phone. If so, you need to know that, too.

To isolate your customer's true objection, probe until you uncover the root of the problem. Probing at this stage will help you avoid the trap that often ensnares the unwary sales rep. That is, your customer responds with, "yes, but…", every time you "answer" an objection. The game goes like this:

Customer:	"I can't afford the system you're talking about."
You:	"My system is a proven time and money saver."
Customer:	"Yes, but my current system works just fine for me."
You:	"Don't forget that your current system costs a lot of staff time."
Customer:	"Yes, but I can't afford time for staff training."

And so on. This verbal volley will continue until annoyance and frustration set in on both sides. No one ever wins this game. Here's how probing can help you control the situation:

Customer:	"I can't afford your system."
You:	"Putting cost aside for a moment, what do you like about the system I've proposed?"
Customer:	"Well, it seems like it might save me time."

You:	"And, how would you use that extra time?"
Customer:	"I might be able to reallocate staff assignments so that we could get the monthly report out without so much overtime."
You:	"What impact would that have on your overall budget?"
Customer:	"Well, for one thing, it would help me get a grip on my payroll."

And so on. Remember to hear your customer out through each response to your probes. And, let your customer know that you have heard and understood – not necessarily accepted – the objection.

Confirm that the objection is real by separating a smokescreen from the true objection. It is simply a matter of probing.

Example 1

You:	"Is that [the objection] the only barrier between you and my product?"
You:	"If I can prove that our delivery schedule will meet your deadline, will you feel comfortable placing your order?"

Example 2

| You: | "Let me see if I understand the situation. You are concerned about our warranty, (restating the objection) is that right?" |

Customer: "Yes."

You: "What concerns you about that?"

Customer: "It's too short."

You: "So if it weren't for the length of our warranty you would be a customer right now. Is that right?" (If they say "Yes", then you have identified the final objection. Then answer it and close the sale.)

Match benefits to your customer's real need and fit your solution to your customer's objection. Once your customer believes that you understand the real objection, he or she will be more receptive to your response. At this point, you'll provide facts, proof and reasons for your customer to buy.

Try the "*feel, felt, found*" technique. For example,

You: "I know how you *feel* and I don't blame you for being skeptical. Actually, other customers have *felt* the same. However, when they investigated the new company further, they *found* that the quality and reliability of service has actually improved since the acquisition."

When blind-sided by an objection, flip the tables by using the reverse technique:

Customer: "I don't think there's much point in taking this any further. We are happy with our current supplier."

You: "That's exactly why I'm here Mr. Customer, to give you the opportunity to evaluate your supplier's competition to confirm that you are getting the best value for your money."

Always ask for the order after you have overcome an objection. There are often several opportunities to close the sale during a sales interview and following an objection is one of the best. Your customer's defenses are down, you have answered all their questions and all they have left to do is make a decision.

You should be prepared for objections. Make a list of Frequently Asked Questions (FAQs). Find answers to the questions and be ready with them. But follow the process - listen, probe and only then, answer and close.

Overcoming the Price Objection

Customers like to buy rationally, analytically, based on the numbers, transaction by transaction, impersonally, with risk built into the price, and with deep product knowledge. However, more often than not, they buy psychologically, based on relationships, without full product knowledge, and with an aversion to risk. Only seven percent of customers do not buy because of price. Claiming price is the deciding factor and convenient for customers because it avoids uncomfortable discussions and it's convenient for you because hearing why someone rejected you is hard. This means that you must avoid giving a price until you are absolutely sure that customers understand all the benefits they are getting. Even then, summarize your proposal before giving the price.

Refer to the price in a positive light, i.e. "an investment". If your price is high, use analogies to a "Harvard education", "a Park Avenue address", "flying First Class", and other premier events. Or products that reinforce the belief that high price equals high quality. Distinguish between price and cost. *Price* is the amount stated on the price tag. *Cost* is price minus savings over the lifespan of the product. The price of a college education may be over $100,000, but because of the higher income college graduates can expect to earn, it costs next to nothing.

Attack the price objection with probing questions such as:

You: "Too high compared to what, Mr. Customer?"

You: "Does that mean that I have failed to demonstrate the value of my proposal or is it that you do not have the budget?"

You: "Do you have a target price in mind - a cost per user, or a fixed price, a licensing agreement?"

You: "Are you comparing our CD/training program/whatever to another program you have purchased...to another, competing proposal?" (If "yes" then ask them to lay it out on the table, to see if it is "apples to apples".)

Sometimes price is a smokescreen for some other issue.

You: "Before we talk more about price, are there any other concerns you may have about our proposal?"

You: "If I could show you how easy it is to cost-justify our program, would you go ahead today?"

You: "Besides price, is there anything else standing in the way of us doing business?"

At other times the price objection is not an objection at all, but a buying signal. They have made up their mind to buy, and now want to negotiate. In that case, close the sale.

You: "Are you ready to move on now and talk money?"

Customer: "Yes."

You: "So I'm safe in assuming that you agree that our proposal solves your problem and that we are capable of executing the agreement?"

Customer: "Yes."

You: "And that our price represents great value?"

Customer: "Good, not great value."

You: "Do you have an order number I should put on my invoice?"

If your customer says "No", explain the value in your pricing. Give them a justification for your price, confirm that they agree and then ask for the order again. If they continue to resist, go back a step or two in the sales process. Return to qualifying. Do the people you are talking to have the money, authority and desire (MAD)? If they have the money, and if they are authorized to spend it, sell them again on your solution to their pain. If they haven't felt the pain, they don't need the solution. If these steps are solid, the close is simply a last step in a logical process.

CHAPTER 9:
GETTING AGREEMENTS
WITH CUSTOMERS

Nothing happens in business until someone sells something

To get agreements from your customer and take some specific action towards the sale, you must build a sense of urgency and momentum. Drive your presentation to a commitment to next steps by responding immediately to buying signals. *Buying signals* are your customers' non-verbal indications that they are ready to make a decision. They can occur anytime in the sales process. It is easy to talk yourself out of a sale by going on well after customers have made up their minds. By talking too much you may trigger an objection, give them time to retract their decision or simply run out of customer time to get a firm agreement. Missing a buying signal does not exactly impress a customer with your responsiveness either.

Closing on Buying Signals

In general, when a customer is considering your proposal, weighing the pros and cons, there is a certain amount of psychological energy being expended. When the customer has made the decision - either for or against your proposal – the tension disappears and the customer relaxes. If you are paying attention, you will see customers release a slight sigh of relief that the decision-making is over. Shoulders may slump, and the body may relax into the chair. When customers really are interested in your product or service, they may touch or stroke the product, pick it up and hold it, glance at it frequently, relax and smile, ask a flurry of questions, ask for details of installation or delivery, ask about payment terms, or warranties, shift from saying "you" to "us" and restate product benefits, or elaborate on how it will solve a problem.

These behaviors may be unconscious signals that the customer is ready to be closed. You should stop what you are doing and ask for the order. Often you will get their agreement. Sometimes it may be premature, but by asking for the order, you will flush out the remaining objections. There is a certain amount of drama associated with closing the sale. It is the moment you and the customer both know is coming. It is the climax of your interactions. Ideally it is the result of increasing momentum and sense of urgency that has been building during the sales process. When you respond to a buying signal by asking customers for a commitment to buy, they experience a mild rush of feelings, which usually causes them to cast down their eyes. When that happens, they must know without a doubt, that when they look up, their eyes will meet yours, unwavering, expectant, and deserving of a straight answer. It may not be the answer you want, but you will get an answer. Be aware that if your eyes are not there, the customer is off the hook and does not have to give you a straight answer.

The old maxim, "The ABCs of Selling – Always Be Closing" is good advice, because you must be receptive to the customer's buying signals and know how to respond appropriately. Since closing means coming to agreement with your customer, you should gain agreements periodically as your call progresses. This gets your customer in the habit of agreeing with you and assures them that both of you are on the same track. Use the ABCs to close on needs. As you probe for and your customers reveal their needs, obtain agreement to confirm your understanding. Make sure that you and your customer both agree on which needs are most important. Later, close on your understanding of the product benefits that match your customer's needs and priorities.

When your customer is ready to buy, make sure you are ready to close. Never let a sales interview run longer than it has to. Even with plenty of information about your product or service, some customers agonize over each detail. Yet these same customers may make a decision in your favor if you are patient and if you persevere.

Since a buying signal indicates that your customer has accepted a benefit of your product and is ready for you to close, you might hear something like - "Well, your proposal sounds O.K." Or an objection, "I need time to think it over." Or silence or a deep sigh. Listen for "I'd buy if I could" message, or the, "That's an interesting proposal" message. The buying signal is often disguised as a question, comment or observation – especially if your customers are trying to hide their feelings. You should be sure that your customer is actually sending a buying signal through the trial close, which reveals any remaining barriers between you and your customer.

Using Closing Techniques

The *Trial Close*, helps you to gain agreement from your customer on an issue that must be resolved before the actual sale. The trial close is a negotiation, a proposed trade. You are proposing that if you were to do something, or agree to something, would your customer be willing to buy your product. For example, "If I can guarantee delivery by the first of the month, will you place your order?" Try this less formulaic way to do a trial close:

You: "On a scale of 1–10, how much do you like the idea?"

Customer: "Eight"

You: "What do we have to do to get a 10?"

If your customer agrees to your trial close, your job is easy. If not, you'll need to retrench and probe to determine what obstacles are still in the way. When you get a clear buying signal, go for the close, using one of the following closing techniques.

The *Summary Close* is best when you've uncovered a number of your customer's needs and proposed a specific solution. It's the close you'll use most often in consultive selling. For example,

You: "Your goal is to reduce overhead by 20 percent next year. You're trying to do that by centralizing your copying services and updating your technology. You have agreed that our proposal does that and more. Let's get the paper work wrapped up and you can start realizing those savings."

In large, complex sales, there are a number of possible intermediate actions that move you closer to the order. Rather than making a traditional close your call objective, identify the next logical agreement you want from your customer that will get your order finalized. For example,

You: "So, a good next step would be for us to get a meeting with your boss to go over these figures."

The *Alternative Close* invites your customer to choose from two or more positive outcomes. You eliminate a negative choice while allowing your customer to feel in control. For example,

> You: "Have you decided on monthly or quarterly billing?"

It's often appropriate to assume that your customer has already made the buying decision and you already have the order. Help your customer get over the difficult hurdle of making the buying decision. The *Assumptive Close* just wraps up the details. You might say, "I'll send that contract over by courier today for your signature." Use this close with every customer. Be very careful of assuming too much or your customer may perceive your close as manipulative or pushy. Remember you earn the right to ask for the order by working hard throughout the sales process. Your customer must be on the brink of a decision for the alternative or assumptive closes to work. For example,

> You: "If you were to go ahead with the service, what would be the first thing you would do after installation? OK, I'll make a note of that and pass it onto our Customer Care people."

> You: "If you were to go ahead with the order, what day of the week would be best for delivery? So I'll schedule your first shipment for 11 AM." (On the day of the week they give you.)

> You: "Will you pay the first installment by check or purchasing card?"

The *Physical Action Close*, as the name implies, invites your customer to make a commitment by initialing, checking off or signing your proposal, or pieces of it. For example,

You:

"Ms. Customer, here is my understanding of your department's information needs. First, you need an in-house, comprehensive and up to date reference library of political and economic information. This would ensure that no longer would anyone make a decision based on inadequate information. And it will spare you the embarrassment of a repeat of the situation involving the CEO you described to me earlier. (Customer nods approvingly. You slide a paper and expensive looking pen across the desk to your customer) OK, would you just put a check mark beside that one for me please?"

Customer:

"OK" (She checks it)

You:

"The second area that needs attention concerns access to information. You felt that all senior executives should have online access to the information. We also recommend that you provide access for all research professionals as well. Our survey indicated that speed and ease of access to information would increase their productivity significantly. Does that make sense?"

Customer:

"Well, of course they would say that, but then on the other hand I appreciate how frequently they need to access the information. Yes, we should definitely consider including them."

You:

(Pointing to the item on the paper, looking expectantly at your customer who picks up the pen and places a check against it) "Thank you".

If your customer agrees to your close, show that you are pleased and appreciate your customer's business. Then, follow your customer's cues. Does he or she want to chat for a while or get right back to work? When the customer signals the end of the call, shake hands, say goodbye and leave. Touch base with your customer again next day and congratulate them on their purchase, reinforcing their belief that they got good value. This helps offset any remorse your customer may be feeling concerning their decision, a fairly common phenomenon among buyers.

If, despite your best efforts, your customer backs out, do not let yourself sound discouraged or frustrated. "No" doesn't necessarily mean "never." Sell your customer on future opportunities. For example, "I just want to let you know that although your answer on this deal is "no", we are interested in doing business with you in the future." And, make a date to review your customer's situation later on. Whatever close you use, remember to use silence as a lever. Ask for the order, and then wait silently for your customer's response – no more selling!

If you have removed all remaining questions from the customer's mind and you have proven the value of your proposition, you have earned the right to ask for the order. Watch for buying signals and close the sale.

CHAPTER 10:
NEGOTIATING WITH CUSTOMERS

Never give, always trade

The old saying, "everything is negotiable", is true in business and in your social and personal life as well. Every day you negotiate with friends and family to sort out who is doing what and when, to arrange a time to pick someone up, to go shopping or to settle who gets the last of the ice-cream. Children are natural negotiators, except that they often favor manipulation and bullying. At work you may negotiate prices and timetables with customers, quotas with your manager, and assistance from support staff. Perhaps you revert to the childhood tactics because you have never learned alternatives. You either push too hard to get the order or give in to your customer's demands too readily. With just a few skills and techniques, and a little knowledge of the principles of negotiation, you can close more deals, help your customers get what they want, and feel good about the process.

Recognizing When Your Customer is Negotiating

When customers are hard-nosed about getting a lower price, 80 percent of the time it is because they do not appreciate the value of your product and have not made a commitment to buy. Step back and re-sell the benefits.

Customer: "You've got to do better than that on price."

You: "I'm glad you mentioned price, Ms. Customer, let's take another look at how our solution is going to save you money/make you money/increase productivity."

Seek a clear agreement from your customer that your solution works before negotiating the price. Make sure that your customer is empowered to do business with you.

Customer: "OK, let's talk price."

You: "Sure. Just so that I'm clear before we move on. We are in agreement that our solution, with the modifications we discussed, is exactly what you are looking for, right?"

Customer: "Well I don't know about that. I've got to run this by my boss."

Never assume that your customer remembers or even understands how much money your solution saves them, or what return they can expect on their investment.

Customer: "I need at least a 20 percent discount."

You: "Why 20 percent, why not 19?"

Customer: "Because there is no way that this is worth the price you are estimating."

You: "That depends on what return you expect on this investment. What do you usually consider as good return – three times, 10 times? Earlier, we estimated that you could get an additional 10% more business from your customers with our solution. I calculated that translates into an additional $5 million, and that's just on your major accounts. Not a bad return on a $100,000 investment don't you think?"

Preparing to Negotiate

Don't underestimate your power in a negotiation. Your relationship with your customer, your understanding of how your proposed solution meets your customer's needs, and your knowledge of the negotiating process itself forms the basis of your power. The more knowledge you have, the broader your power base. For example, you may know the limits of your ability to discount price. But do you also know how much room you have to maneuver with delivery schedules, product quantity or quality, and payment terms? If you do not, you may lose the deal, or win the deal but lose your profit margin. You and your customers may decide to negotiate price, but you may forget to negotiate terms, conditions, delivery schedules, resources, ownership, work location, time and scope.

You may have a variety of objectives in a negotiation. Sometimes you may want to "buy" your way into your customer account by delivering at cost, because this one is a cornerstone customer. Other times, you may want to demonstrate to your buyer that the days of "off the rate card pricing" are over. Or, because there is a large backlog of orders, you must hold the line on delivery times but give a little on payment terms.

Always get what you want from a sale by being prepared to negotiate. Do not be taken by surprise when your customer ends the meeting just as you are about to ask for the order, or when they want to revisit the price after a handshake agreement. You will always be prepared to negotiate successfully if you have thought about what would be your best outcome, beforehand, the most likely outcome and the worst outcome. Knowing your bottom line also enhances your confidence in negotiating. This is the most critical part of preparation. If you do not know your best outcome, do not expect to get it. Conversely, if you are not clear about your minimal acceptable outcome, you may regret it. Also determine your customer's best case, most likely case, and least acceptable case.

Prevent your feelings from interfering with your effectiveness by calculating your bottom line before you get into an emotionally charged negotiation. Consider this scenario, reported by The New Yorker magazine. You are sitting on a park bench with a stranger. A Consultant comes up and offers both of you $10. The stranger gets to decide how the money should be divided. You get to veto the division, but if you do, neither of you gets anything. Good sense says take any division, even a dollar. But most people reject offers of less than three dollars. Reason? Their pride interferes with their good sense.

Customers often make initial flat demands. They may say, "We've got to have Phase One finished by Thursday." A little probing might reveal the drivers of that position and uncover the real need. Maybe your customer wants to report completion of Phase One at a regular meeting with his boss. Or perhaps your customer is under the mistaken belief that it takes you two days to turnaround a report on Phase One or perhaps he is expecting push back from you and wants to give himself some cushion. A critical skill throughout the sales process, probing is especially critical to get past this first round negotiating gambit.

Consider this example. Two little girls come home from school, running into the kitchen and heading straight to the refrigerator. They begin to fight over who gets the one and only orange. Mother intervenes, and what does she do? Cuts it in half, of course, and gives the girls half each. One little girl hungrily devours her half, tossing the rind in the garbage. The other girl fishes out the rind from the garbage, peels her half and throws out the fruit. Armed with the rind of the orange she proceeds to use it for a craft project for homework.

In this scenario, the girls' initial demands were that they had to have the orange and had it not been for Mom's intervention they may have gone to war over it. Mom did what you may well have done yourself to settle the negotiation. She took the easy way out and forced a compromise. Had she done a little probing, she would have learned that the girls' real needs were not the same. One wanted the fruit and the other wanted the rind. The girls allowed their feelings to interfere with their effectiveness. They perceived the situation as a threat and they became afraid that they might not get what they wanted. That fear impaired their judgment concerning how to resolve the issue and drove them into a confrontation.

To sweeten a negotiation, you may offer your customer a series of seminars in a technical issue, delivered by your best engineer. Overall the seminar goes well but there are complaints about sexism from some participants. Your customer demands that you replace the engineer. However, you have no other engineers available. After some back and forth you and your customer agree that your engineer will apologize to the seminar participants and will register for a course in diversity awareness. You further offer to be present during the remaining seminars yourself.

An instinctive response to negotiating is to protect your ground and aim to win the negotiation, as though there can only be a winner and a loser. In fact, several outcomes are possible along two different lines. There will be an outcome for the *substance* of the deal itself, (i.e. the terms, conditions, price etc.) and there will be an outcome concerning your *relationship* with your customer. Most of the time the substance of the deal will be as important to you as strengthening your customer relationship. You will want repeat business from your customer. There will be times when the substance of the deal is very important to you, but you do not expect to, or do not want do business with this customer again. Perhaps you can make a bundle of money on a deal but your customer's business practices are so distasteful to you that you decide that this is the only deal you will do with them.

A *win-win* outcome occurs when you and your customer both get what you want. Win-win is your goal when negotiating with a customer who you want to do business with repeatedly, and where the substance of the deal is important to you. Often win-win outcomes require that you use empathy and probing skills to find a creative solution to the problem of different and mutually exclusive wants.

A *win-lose* outcome occurs when you get what you want but your customer is less than satisfied. Win-lose is your best approach when you do not trust your customer to play by the rules. You don't expect to do business with them again and the substance of the deal is very important to you.

Lose-win is when your customer gets the better of you, an outcome that is rarely desirable except in those instances where your relationship with your customer is very important to you but the substance of the deal is not.

Finally, a *Lose/Lose* outcome occurs when neither of you gets all of what you want. You compromise so that you both get some, but not all of what you want. Typically, compromise is used to resolve a difference in price by splitting the difference. In this respect, compromise is a lose/lose outcome. You and your customer may agree to compromise for the sake of harmony, convenience, to avoid uncomfortable conflict or because neither the substance nor the relationship is important. For example, at a garage sale you might compromise because you don't really need that table and you probably won't see the seller again. You might brag about getting a good deal but in fact you have not because you had to compromise. Compromising is the easy way out, and not the hallmark of a truly authentic sales person, whereas *creative problem-solving* is challenging and is the way to a win-win outcome. To minimize the temptation to compromise, state your intentions clearly upfront.

> You: "Ms. Customer, my intention is to negotiate a solution that works for you and works for me as well. At this early stage I do not have such a solution. However, I am confident that if we are both committed to a win/win outcome, if we are fair and reasonable, if we talk more about what we want and explore some creative avenues, then that win/win will present itself."

This kind of statement has the added benefit of reducing any defensiveness your customer may have towards the negotiation. Assume good faith, fair play and expect fairness. Assume that your customers are trustworthy, operate with good intentions and are honest until proven otherwise. Customers may be guarded and they may even be defensive, but they may still want to operate in good faith. A little listening, probing and empathizing, while agreeing to nothing, can help determine good faith.

Trust improves negotiation outcomes. Take the time to build a relationship with your customer before negotiating. If your customers get to know you, they are more likely to trust you. And if they trust you, you are more likely to get win-win outcomes.

Never Give, Always Trade

Now you are ready to move into the fun part of negotiating – trading. Start high and make your first proposal sound like your last. If your customer does not accept it, express your disappointment. An effective way to convey this is to flinch and cast your eyes down for a moment. Then re-commit to a win/win outcome. Take one issue at a time, starting with the easiest. Starting with the easiest issue allows you and your customer to achieve an early success, and to have some common agreements to build on.

Float a tentative solution, using the formula, "If you will, then I will." Never give, always trade. This trial solution should include a concession from you, at a cost of a concession from your customer. At this point, your concession should not be a major one; it should be somewhere between your best-case outcome and your most likely case outcome.

Slow down your breathing, use deliberate gestures and facial expressions, keep your head up and look your customer directly in the eyes. This helps you maintain control of the negotiating process. If your customer counter-offers, once again flinch and allow some disappointed silence to fall. Continue this process until your customer agrees.

Move on to the next issue, remembering to save the toughest issue to last. Never indicate impatience. You want your customer to believe that if necessary to gain agreement, you can do this all day. Keep in mind that feelings prefer immediate gratification to long term gain, even when the long term gain is greater. If you are anxious during a negotiation, you may make concessions to relieve the anxiety. If you are calm, you are more likely to take the long view and trade rather than concede.

Throughout the process, confirm and record agreements, no matter how small. You should also show appreciation whenever your customer adheres to the ground rules. When all the issues have been settled, summarize and record the outcomes. Follow up with written confirmation of your agreements with your customer, again complimenting them on their respect for the ground rules.

Sometimes your customer may want to ratify your negotiated outcome, usually by having their boss sign off on the agreement. If this is the case, note it in writing, "subject to ratification." This also implies that you can re-open negotiation of any of the issues if sign-off becomes a problem.

Countering Customer Negotiation Tactics

Be prepared for customer negotiating tactics by determining your response before your sales meeting. Don't be blindsided into giving away something you did not intend to. Your customers may attempt to improve their outcome at your expense (lose-win). *Negotiating tactics* tend to turn the focus away from legitimate, negotiable items and ask for concessions based on irrelevant issues. Sometimes negotiation tactics are used unconsciously (see examples below). Tactics have persisted and are touted in some negotiation books and training workshops because they are effective, at least in the short-term. Their long-term effect is to hinder relationship building because your customer does not want to feel that you are taking unfair advantage.

It is amazing how many concessions you make when flattered. It feels so good to be praised that you want to thank the person, and what better way than to give them what they want. Resist the impulse to be a "people pleaser" and stay firm.

Customer: "Would you do me favor? Just add this question to the survey? I'd do it myself except that *you are so much better at it than* I am."

You: "Thanks for that. Normally I'd be happy to do it, but unfortunately it's too late. The survey has gone to printing."

Watch out for the "*Poor innocent me*" ploy, sometimes used unconsciously. Empathy when teamed with firm resistance, again wins the day.

Customer: "This has been the week from hell. I've had extra projects dumped on me, my wife is having surgery Monday and my car is in the shop as a result of an accident. Could you do me a big favor and not charge me for X?"

You: "Believe me, I know exactly how you feel. I've had days like that too. I wish I could help but we have already agreed on a price for X."

You have come to an agreement, have it documented, perhaps even ratified and all that is left to do is get signatures. With pen poised to sign, your customer pauses, points to an item, usually the price, and says "How about knocking another 5% off and I'll sign this immediately?" From where he sits, what does he have to lose by *escalating demands*? In your haste to close, you just might cave in. The correct response here is simply "no".

If you want to disagree with your customers, mention your reasons first (or they may not get listened to). If they are accepted, you may not have to point out that you disagree. To make your point, use benchmarks such as standard operating procedures, or professional standards rather than opinion or speculation. Don't rebut every point your customer makes, even if you are convinced your customer is wrong. If you feel that you must launch an attack on your customer, do it abruptly, rather than building up to it in a way that allows them time to develop a counter attack.

Customers may try to get a lower price by asking for a breakdown of your system's components and then trying to negotiate a lower price, component by component, or by putting out to bid individual components. Similar to the escalating demands tactic, at the last minute, the customer tries to return to an item agreed to earlier and tries to open it up again for negotiation. The hope is that by creating confusion, they will be able to get a better deal on the current item.

Customer: "You guys are tough. This is still more than I would like to pay. What is the breakdown and how much do you pay for labor? How much for overhead? What if I bought …?"

You: "Mr. Customer, I'm confused. Earlier you agreed on the total budget and that it represented outstanding value. By your own calculations, you expect a 10:1 return. And that's what really important here, isn't it? Not my costs. So, what day is best for your kick-off meeting, Thursday or Friday?"

Escalating authority is a classic tactic that attempts to get you to make concessions, especially on price, by claiming that your proposal has to go to a higher level because it is 10% or 5% higher than the "company guidelines." The hope here is that you will be reluctant to, in effect, start all over again with someone else and will make the concession. The "company guideline" might well be fictional.

"*What if I bought …*" is a tactic similar to the escalating demands tactic. At the last minute, your customer tries to return to an item agreed to earlier and tries to open it up again for negotiation. The hope is that by creating confusion, she will be able to get a better deal on the current item.

You: "Ms. Customer, sorry, but I'm confused. We agreed to that item yesterday, and in fact, at the time you seemed to be pretty pleased with the solution. Has something changed? If not, let's move on. We're on a roll here."

Walk away and wait is another effective tactic when your customer senses you would like to close as soon as possible. Your customer abruptly brings the meeting to an end, without responding to your proposal. Your phone calls are not returned, no email, sometimes for weeks. The hope is that you will assume that your price is too high, and when you eventually re-establish contact, that you will have already lowered it. Be patient. Stay in touch, continuing to show your interest but not your anxiety, in resolving the issue or closing the deal. Conversely, don't immediately make a counter proposal when your customer makes an offer. Remember everything is negotiable, including arbitrary deadlines for a response.

CHAPTER 11:
SUMMARY AND NEXT STEPS

A journey of a thousand miles begins with one step

— *Chinese proverb*

Now that you have read this book take some time to reflect on what you have learned that will improve your selling. You probably picked up this book because you want to become a better sales person, even if you were not sure that this book would help. In fact, you won't all have learned the same things. Some of you will close the book feeling validated. You are already well down this path and doing many of the things you must do to remain successful in the global age. Others may be experiencing some mild shock. Perhaps your customers have not increased their demands on you, or they have and your response is less effective than you would like. However you are encouraged because you have picked up some ideas and skills. Others still may retain a healthy skepticism, and hopefully not cynicism, about the recommendations in this book.

In any case the next step is up to you. You are responsible for your own professional development. Not your sales manager, or your sales trainer or human resources or your spouse or friends. You must take charge and one step at a time make the changes you know you must make to become a more authentic sales person and prepare yourself for the ongoing evolution of the marketplace. Fortunately there are excellent tools available and you do not have to do it alone.

Start by tackling the improvement that will yield the best return on your investment of time and effort. Perhaps you simply need to listen better for the larger business opportunities, or build a more authentic relationship with a customer who has high profit potential. Whatever it is, strengthen your commitment to it by putting it in writing. Try to identify the next opportunity you will have to try the new approach. It may be with a particular customer next week, or it may be the first time a particular issue arises with any customer that calls for a different response. Put that next opportunity in writing, too.

Now consider what you must do to keep the momentum going in your professional development. Perhaps you can sit down with your sales manager or good friend and outline what you want tot do and ask for their support. Their support might be as little as asking you occasionally how you are doing with your attempts to improve, or they might provide you with regular coaching sessions, or secure the funding for a training course or educational program.

 In the meantime you must practice the skills you wish to acquire so that they become automatic and fully integrated into your authentic self. It's not enough to say to yourself that you get it, that you understand that you can probably do it. A surgeon does not walk into an operating theater intending to try a new surgical technique that he/she just finished reading. At the peak of his game, Tiger Woods practices 10 hours a day between tournaments. You can practice selling skills through role plays with your manager or colleagues. You can test out new ideas by exploring them within your team or company, before landing them on the desk of your customer. Find out how you really feel about the ideas in this book by informally debating them with your manager or colleagues.

Whatever you do, monitor your energy and enthusiasm for sales. They are both absolutely necessary for success. If you sense that they are flagging take action immediately to get to the root cause. Again, find someone with whom you can talk about it. (Your mind is like a bad neighborhood, you should not go in there alone.) Usually talking about it is enough to turn the corner. However, if you cannot maintain a high level of energy and enthusiasm despite getting help, there is no shame in accepting that it may be time for a career change. Let us hope not, because sales is an honorable and rewarding career and one that our economic system depends heavily on. There is no limit to the amount of financial success you can have in sales and no end to the amount of satisfaction you can get by selling through your authentic self.

INDEX

SOURCES AND RESOURCES

Harrison Monarth and Larina Kase, *The Confident Speaker*, McGraw-Hill, 2007

Interpersonal Development, LLC . http://www.interpersonaldevelopment.com

John Le Carre, *The Secret Pilgrim*, Ballantine Books, 2001

John Cassidy, *Mind Games*, The New Yorker, September 18, 2006

JustSell.com http://www.justsell.com/

Larry Newman, *Proposal Guide for Business and Technical Professionals*, Third Edition, Shipley Associates/Logistics Specialists Inc. 2006

Sally Bibb and Jeremy Kourdi, *Trust Matters for organizational and personal success*. Palgrave Macmillan, 2004

United States Professional Sales Association. http://www.upsa-intl.org/

Social Styles Model™ by TRACOM Group. www.tracomgroup.com

28369636R00104

Made in the USA
San Bernardino, CA
07 March 2019